Psychological Yearbook

Vol. 2, 1995

Psychological Yearbook

University of Copenhagen

Vol. 2 · 1995

Edited by

*Niels Engelsted, Judy Gammelgaard,
Anker Helms Jørgensen, Simo Køppe, Aksel Mortensen*

MUSEUM TUSCULANUM PRESS
1996

Psychological Yearbook Vol. 2, 1995.
© Museum Tusculanum Press 1996
Composition by Ole Klitgaard, set in Palatino
Paste-up of illustrations by Bente Jarlhøj
Printed in Denmark by Bogtrykkeriet, Skive
ISSN 1395 0878
ISBN 87 7289 368 0

Published with the support of
The Faculty for the Humanities, University of Copenhagen

MUSEUM TUSCULANUM PRESS
University of Copenhagen
Njalsgade 92
DK-2300 Copenhagen S.
Denmark

TABLE OF CONTENTS

Foreword 7

Gretty M. Mirdal: The psycho-biology of asthma 9

Sven Mørch: Young adults – Problems and research perspectives 25

Ole Elstrup: A Strategy for the Development of a Theory of
    Organizational Leadership and Administration 53

Erik Schultz: Dream and Neuroses 81

Reinhard Stelter: Identity, Self-Concept and Sport 89

Morten Nissen: Psycho-social practice 93

Bjarne Pedersen: The works of Kurt Goldstein 95

Publications 1994-1995 97

Foreword

In 1994 the current publication *Psychological Yearbook – University of Copenhagen* was launched in order to present the Copenhagen-Psychology tradition to a wider international audience and thereby stimulate communication and collaboration across borders. We hope the reader enjoyed volume 1. We hereby present volume 2, encompassing some major contributions from 1995.

Like volume 1, the current volume witnesses a feature of the Copenhagen-Psychology tradition, deeply rooted in experimental and phenomenological traditions, namely *multiplicity*. Thus, the first papers cover three quite diverse areas: Health Psychology, Social Psychology, and Organisational Psychology.

The opening contribution by Gretty Mirdal – a Doctor Phil. thesis – investigates the interconnections between emotional, cognitive, physiological and environmental factors in the course of the disease of asthma. Based on a longitudinal study of 20 women, Gretty Mirdal suggests that the paths between "body and mind" should be conceived of as multidirectional and and as interrelated through open, permeable systems – rather than merely two-directional as is often the case.

Sven Mørch reports on young adults from the perspective of Social Psychology. His starting point is the need to look at both the process of individualisation and the possibilities and problems in becoming an adult in modern society. Drawing on previous research, on post-modernism and on activity theory, he establishes some elements of an activity youth theory.

The topic of the next paper by Ole Elstrup Rasmussen is leadership. He proposes a strategy for developing a theory of leadership, drawing upon cognitive psychology and text analysis. The distinction between qualifications and competence plays a key role in the exposition.

The next paper illustrates the secondary aim of *Psychological Yearbook – University of Copenhagen*: to elucidate the history of the Copenhagen-Psychology tradition. Erik Schultz reviews the book Dream and Neurosis by Franz From, one of the most influential researchers in psychology in Denmark. The book was published in Danish in 1944 and has been revised and reprinted several times. As the book contains points of view still highly relevant, it was translated into English in order to make it available to the international audience. Erik Scultz's review focuses on three concepts in Franz From's attempt at bridging between cognition and the unconscious: Universalia, Identialia, and Generalia.

The volume concludes with three short presentations of the Ph.D. dissertations from 1995: Richard Stelter on athletes' identity and self-concepts, Morten Nissen on development projects in psycho-social work, and Bjarne Pedersen on the works of the neuropsychologist Kurt Goldstein.

Aksel Mortensen   *Judy Gammelgaard*
Head of Psychological Laboratory   Head of Institute of Clinical Psychology

The psychobiology of asthma:
On the relationship between bronchial and emotional hypersensitivity

GRETTY M. MIRDAL

The roots

Respiration is the basis of life. It marks the beginning and the end of our existence, and shortness of breath brings asthma patients nearer to these limits than most other people. Life and death run naturally as recurrent themes in the lives of persons afflicted with any severe disease, but even more so when the impairment, as in asthma, is so intimately tied to breathing.

The very word "breath" is related to the living body and mind, encompassing both **respiration** (that which gives the body life: "No warmth, no *breath*, shall testify thou livest"[1]), and **spirit** (in the sense of mind, thoughts, words and feelings: "if words be made of *breath*, and *breath* of life, I have no life to *breathe*"[2]). This double meaning of breath is not particular to English, but can be found in other languages, such as "ånd/ånde" in the Nordic and "nefes" in the Semitic languages. As a matter of fact, the word "spirit" is at the root of the Latin "respirare". Persons who suffer from recurring asthma attacks thus acquire a special knowledge both of the borderland between life and death, and of the interaction between body and mind. They are, so to speak, experts in psychosomatics, and were therefore selected as informants in the present project, with the aim of studying the interaction between psychological and biological processes as they manifest themselves in asthma.

---

[1] Shakespeare, Romeo and Juliet, Act 4, Scene 1
[2] Shakespeare, Hamlet, Act 3, Scene 4

Throughout history, each epoch has dealt with the body-mind problem on the basis of the cultural and scientific premises of the particular time. Recent research in developmental, cognitive, clinical and neuropsychology provides a renewed frame of reference for a reinterpretation of some of the earlier conceptions of the interactions between body and mind, between psyche and soma. It is in this context that asthma was selected as the topic of the present project.

The psychosomatic aspects of hypersensitivity

Words like irritability, intolerance, and oversensitivity are often used in relation to both bodily and mental reactions. Sensitivity denotes both the tenderness of a healing wound and the touchiness of a person who is easily hurt. Hypersensitivity, in turn, signals a tendency to receive and to respond to stimuli with unusual keenness, both at the physical and at the psychological level. Is this use of identical terms for physical and mental phenomena due to a correspondence between them? Are we indeed dealing with two manifestations of the same phenomenon, or is it a linguistic insufficiency, a paucity of words for physical and mental states, that misleads us into believing that there is an equivalence between physical hypersensitivity (e.g., an allergy) and emotional oversensitivity?

One of the aims of my project, and the one that will be developed in this article, has been to study such possible correspondences and interactions between psychological and biological oversensitivity. Asthma is a disease related to **hypersensitivity** and **hyperreactivity** of the bronchi. Since the time of Hippocrates it has, however, also been considered as a disease particularly susceptible to emotional influences.

The **bronchial hyperreactivity** which characterizes asthma is provoked either by **allergens** (e.g., pollen, animal hair, house dust, and the like) or by **irritants**, (e.g., smoke or air pollution which provoke irritation in both normal and hyperreactive persons, the latter tending to react more strongly to weaker stimulation). Asthma is thus related to an oversensitivity[3] of the airways which causes muscular constriction, increased mucus production, inflammation of lung tissue and edema mediated by immune system reactions. These processes provoke in turn the typical symptoms of asthma: coughing, breathlessness, tightness in the chest, and wheezing.

---

[3] The terms sensitivity and sensibility are used synonymously in this article.

In psychology, **oversensitivity** refers to an increased sensibility, and **hyperreactivity** to an increased reaction to a stimulus that is weaker and less persistent than normally required to arouse an emotional reaction. In Shand's classical "study of the emotions and sentiments" from 1920, sensibility/sensitivity to an emotion is defined as the degree and the manner in which it responds to its appropriate stimuli. When sensitivity is increased, so too is the speed, intensity and duration of the response, and the degree to which it occurs in connection to a weaker stimulus. More recent studies of emotional hypersensibility focus on specific symptoms and on a more restricted range of emotions and behaviour than the earlier studies (e.g. feeling critical of others, being easily hurt, feeling inferior to others, feeling others are unfriendly, etc.). Hypersensitivity in both the bronchial and the emotional area is thus characterized by the same quality, *in casu* an exaggerated reaction in relation to the stimulus that provokes it.

If the two kinds of hypersensitivity and hyperreactivity (i.e., the bronchial and the emotional) are related as hypothesized here, then asthma patients (who by definition are hyperreactive at the bronchial level) should also manifest signs of hypersensitivity and hyperreactivity at the emotional level. Before describing the study in which this hypothesis was investigated, it might be useful to give a short critical review of the current literature in the field of psychosomatics, and to present the theoretical assumptions which have been developed by the present author, and on which this particular study has been based.

Psychosomatics: past and present

Asthma has been the subject of a large number of psychological investigations, albeit for other reasons and with other purposes than those mentioned above. The vast majority of these studies, many of which were conducted from a psychodynamic perspective, aimed at revealing the psychological antecedents of asthma, looking for its causes either in 1) early mother-child relations (see Weiner, 1977 for a review) and family dynamics (e.g., Minuchin, 1978, Wilson, 1989), and/or in 2) intrapsychic conflicts or deficits in the personality structure of so-called "psychosomatic patients" (e.g., Alexander et al., 1968, McDougall, 1982, Taylor, 1987). This literature is analyzed in the book, "Åndenød"[4], (Mirdal, 1994) that was published on the present study and will not be reviewed in this article in any detail. There are, however, certain issues raised by these earlier studies which have influenced both the questions I have proposed to investigate and the methods that were used to this end. I shall mention some of these issues here, firstly in relation to psychoanalytic literature, and then in connection to the literature on stress.

The early studies on the psychological etiology of asthma were mostly retrospective, i.e., they assessed the importance of psychological factors in the etiology of the disease long after its manifestation. However, by the time the illness has manifested itself, it is no longer possible to determine whether the personality traits, habits and life style of the patient are causes or results of the disease.

An area where this problem has been most aggravating is in the alleged role of the mother-child relation in the development of the disease. For example, the term "psychosomatogenic mother" was coined to designate domineering, ambivalent and invading mothers who were thought to be responsible for their child's condition. The reverse, that is, **the effect of the child's asthma on the mother's feelings and behaviour, has been almost totally ignored**. Similarly, the fact that the anxiety engendered by not being able to breathe might arouse attachment patterns on the part of the child, independently of the mother's personality or care-taking style, has not received any attention.

Curiously enough, the characteristics attributed to the mothers of asthmatic patients are also found in archetypal descriptions of "the bad mother" in relation to many other physical and mental disorders, as if the fact of having had such a mother was a sufficient explanation for the occurrence of any misfortune or any disease throughout a person's life. It seems that this school of thought has taken an implicit image of "the perfect mother" as a yardstick: the comparison group used in the research on the mothers of asthmatic children has not been "control mothers" or "good-enough mothers", but "perfect mothers".

The third problem area to be mentioned here concerning the psychoanalytic literature on the subject is that **asthma has been, almost by definition, regarded as a "psychosomatic disorder"**, as a disease of psychological

---

[4] "Åndenød" is composed of 1) *ånd*=breath/ *ånde*=spirit and 2) *nød*=distress, want, destitution. It can be translated as **shortness of breath** or difficult breathing, but "åndenød" implies a spiritual distress which these english expressions do not convey. "**Respiratory distress**" seems therefore to be a more adequate translation of the Danish title of the book.

origin, the implication being that all cases of asthma are caused by psychological problems. This assumption is obviously inadmissible in the light of the well-established multifactorial etiology of the disease. As a matter of fact, the whole concept of "psychosomatic disorder", the idea that some somatic diseases are by definition psychological in origin, is no longer tenable. Actually, neither "psychosomatic disorders" nor "psychophysiological disorders" appear in the latest version of the American Psychiatric Association's Diagnostic and Statistical Manual (DSM-IV). Psychological factors affecting a medical condition are now listed under "conditions that may be a focus of clinical attention". The implication of this change of attitude is of course, that thoughts and emotions naturally affect many somatic conditions without this being considered as a sign of mental disorder.

My conclusion, drawn from the review of the psychodynamically oriented literature on asthma, was that the psychoanalytic method can help to disclose the ways in which a patient's thoughts, emotions and interpersonal relations influence and are influenced by his/her disease. It provides a method of exploration and reconstruction of the individual asthma patient's life history. However, these merits of the **psychoanalytic method of treatment** do not constitute a validation of **psychoanalytic theories**. The success of the treatment may be due to many other factors than the therapist's theoretical background.

Furthermore, since psychoanalysts report that their treatment leads to successful results despite the different psychoanalytic schools' seemingly contradictory assumptions on the nature of the so-called psychosomatic diseases (i.e. neurotic vs. borderline personality), it is justified to question the validity of these theoretical assumptions.

In contrast to psychoanalysis, cognitive approaches to psychosomatic reactions and stress research have their roots in academic rather than clinical traditions. Stress research has generally been interdisciplinary, involving disciplines such as experimental and behavioral psychology, neurology and physiology. Apart from elucidating some of the physiological processes related to psychological phenomena, this research has led to a change in the very definition of the field of psychosomatic disorders by illustrating how stress and negative feelings affect, both specifically and generally, many different functions of the organism. This being so, there was no longer any reason for restricting the field of psychosomatics to a limited number of diseases, e.g., asthma, eczema, rheumatoid arthritis, hypertension, ulcerative colitis, peptic ulcer and thyrotoxicosis, the so-called "classical psychosomatic disorders". It is due to this change that any bodily disease which can be related to psychological factors, either in its onset or course, is now regarded as psychosomatic, and no one disease is by definition more so than any other. This viewpoint has, as mentioned above, now been adopted in the main international classifications of disorders, e.g., DSM-IV and ICD-10.

Stress research brought about a second important change in the conception of body-mind interactions. It focused on environmental and social stressors, in contrast to the psychoanalytic emphasis on intrapsychic phenomena. Research on the detrimental consequences of negative life events on health contributed indirectly to a redefinition of **psychological influences**, i.e., to changes in the very conception of the term "psychological": the scope of possible psychological factors influencing health and disease, which had been restricted mainly to intrapsychic conflicts, was now enlarged to include a broad range of personality traits, stressing life conditions and situations.

The criticism that could be directed toward stress research includes: 1) the lack of importance given to the individual characteristics of the person experiencing the stressful event, and 2) the overextension of the concept of stress to include any change in the environment demanding adaptation on the part of the organism; similarly, the word "coping" came to cover the entire range of possible emotions, thoughts and actions, with which an individual can react to stress. When concepts are so broadly defined they lose their usefulness and thereby become uninteresting.

In spite of the widespread criticism of the concepts of "stress" and "coping" for their lack of precision, they are difficult to avoid, both because they are well-established in psychology, and because they have become a part of both patients' and physicians' vocabulary. Recent endeavours to integrate cognitive and psycho-dynamic approaches have, however, brought more meaningful dimensions to stress research, by emphasizing the significance of the individual's appraisal of the situation, his/her past history and personality characteristics as well as possibilities of taking action and maintaining control.

The theoretical background of the present study: The developmental aspects of psychosomatic regulation

The model of psychosomatic regulation which is used in this study is based on some of the above-mentioned psychodynamic and cognitive psychological theories, as well as on the present author's earlier research on premature and full-term infants. Because the organism of the new-born infant is relatively less complex than the adult's, it is easier to see the precursors of psychosomatic interactions in the early stages of life. Even premature infants exhibit signs of *psychosomatic disorganization* when they are under stress (e.g., noise, light, medical interventions, etc.), and of *reorganization* when they receive adequate stimulation.

At the **physiological level**, the disorganization manifests itself in changes in, e.g., temperature, respiration, and visceral reactions: At the **level of the motor system**, in hyper- or hypotonicity. Stressors also affect the modulation of the **state system** by inhibiting attention (state system refers in this context to states of consciousness ranging from deep sleep through attention to motoric activity and crying). All of these changes within the organism, and especially changes in attentiveness, affect in turn the infant's receptiveness and interactions with the caregiver (**the interactional system**).

New-born infants, even when they are premature, have some capacity for self-regulation. Obviously, the younger and the more vulnerable the infant is, the more dependent he will be on a caregiver in order to achieve this regulation. These intersystemic and interpersonal processes in the first months of life have been conceptualized, among others by Als (1979). Her spiral model has been a source of inspiration in the present study (see fig. 1). I have here extended her model to include emotional and cognitive processes that develop beyond the earliest stages of life, e.g., the differentiation and modulated control of emotional expression, of cognitive schemata, of linguistic expression, and of problem solving.

Figure 1.
Model of Expanding Infant Organization Within Infant-Caregiver System

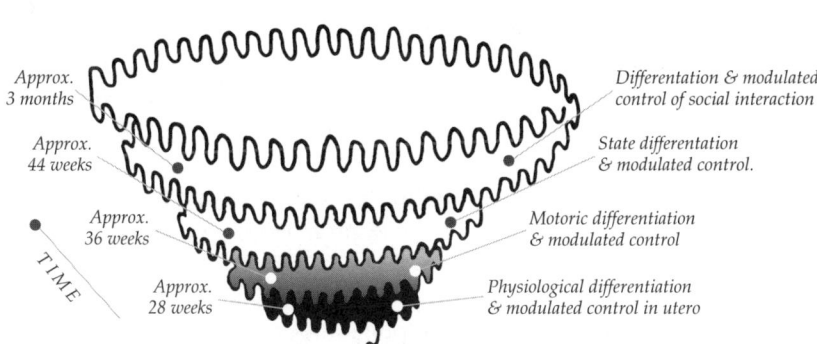

Applied to asthma, the spiral could be used as a model for both upward and downward effects on organizing and disorganizing processes, as in the following example: upon exposure to an allergy-provoking agent, e.g. house dust, an asthmatic child might begin to have difficulties in breathing (disorganization at the physiological level), which affect his posture and muscle tonus (at the muscular and motoric level), entailing a change in attentional capacity at the level of state regulation (vigilance, frustration tolerance, etc.), which in turn influences his ability to interact with his environment and disrupts possible social interactions.

Reciprocally, an appropriate intervention on the part of a responsive and responsible adult at an early stage of this disorganization spiral may start a reorganization process, which can then either stop further disorganization or even start a process of reorganization. This theoretical model of interaction between the physiological, motor, cognitive, emotional and social systems is throughout the present study "filled out", concretized, and illustrated with data collected from asthma patients.

Description of the study

The aim of the present study has consequently been to investigate and substantiate the continuous interconnections between emotional, cognitive, physiological and environmental factors in the course of the disease, and not to uncover "the psychological factors behind asthma". To this end, it seemed necessary to study the individual patients' subjective experience of 1) how thought and emotions affected breathing, and vice versa, 2) the antecedents and consequents of the disease, and 3) the factors that could aggravate or ameliorate their condition.

It was the present author's conviction that valid and meaningful information on such private, complex questions can only be obtained on the basis of good co-operation between patient and researcher, a prolonged period of data collection, and a sustained relationship of mutual confidence and respect. Psychotherapy was for these reasons chosen as the most suitable method of data collection for this project.

Female patients who were affiliated to the Allergy Unit of the University Hospital of Copenhagen between 1990 and 1992, and who met the following selection criteria were offered the possibility of participating in this study: moderate asthma, no other serious diseases, age between 25 and 45, regular menstrual cycles, no sign of pregnancy, no participation in other studies or alternative treatments that might interfere with the present project, and willingness to engage in psychotherapy for a period of six months. The psychotherapy was conducted by the present author on an individual basis, and founded on psycho-dynamic and cognitive principles.

The research population consisted of 20 women, 10 in the treatment group, and 10 in a control group that received the customary medical treatment but no psychological therapy. Only women were included in the study for the purpose of studying the effects of menstruation on psychological and bronchial hyperreactivity. The mean age of the patients was 35 in the first and 31 in the second group. The mean number of sessions was 15.7. (The control group was established with the purpose of assessing the effect of psychotherapy on asthma patients. This part of the study is not included in the present article and will therefore not be described any further. The results can be obtained from the author.)

The combination of psychotherapy and research had both advantages and disadvantages that are discussed at length in "Åndenød", (Mirdal, 1994). The method's main disadvantage was that clinical concern for the individual patient interfered with the use of standardized procedures. Moreover, the very lengthy involvement with each patient limited the number of subjects who could participate in the study. On the other hand, the data that were collected in this way were more refined, more subtle and faceted than information collected through questionnaires or interviews. Furthermore, the patients were considered as co-researchers in the investigation of the psychosomatic aspects of their own illness, and thereby motivated to engage more actively in both research and treatment.

The assessment of hypersensitivity

As mentioned above, bronchial hyperreactivity is defined as a stronger reaction than normally expected to allergens and/or irritants which provoke similar but weaker reactions in healthy persons. Similarly, the term psychological hyperreactivity is used here to imply a lower threshold for certain types of emotional stressors which affect a person more strongly than they would if they occurred at periods of lesser vulnerability.

The diagnosis of **bronchial hypersensitivity** rests primarily on 1) the identification of possible allergens or irritants (e.g., dust, animal fur, feathers, various food), 2) the identification of affected organ(s) (e.g., skin, airways, eyes), 3) the description of the type of reaction in the affected area (e.g., secretion of tears, itching of the eyes, swelling of the eyelids), and 4) the assessment of the intensity of the reaction.

In contrast to the immunological/bronchial area, where it is possible to set objective criteria for the above-mentioned four areas of hypersensitivity and hyperreactivity, the definition of **emotional oversensitivity** is mostly subjective, both with respect to the very experience and its intensity, and with respect to the limit between sensitivity and oversensitivity. Can one be too sensitive? Are the terms sensitivity, receptiveness, susceptibility, irritability and touchiness synonymous? Where does sensitivity end and hypersensitivity begin? And who sets the limits of desirability and acceptability? The assessment of psychological hypersensitivity was therefore one of the main difficulties in designing the study.

The assessment in both the bronchial and immunological areas had to deal with similar methodological problems, e.g., 1) test-retest reliability (the same patients may react differently to the same provoking factor, and present various thresholds of tolerance at different times); 2) diversities between patients and doctors in the identification of provoking agents in either allergological or emotional contexts[5], and 3) the fact that the oversensitivity, be it allergological or psychological, can manifest itself in many different ways, the same provoking agent causing different symptoms in different persons, or even in the same person at different times.

Just as hazel nuts may induce a variety of different conditions such as asthma, eczema, hay fever, urticaria or migraine, the same stressful event (e.g., separation from a loved one) may provoke a variety of emotions such as sadness, depression, anger, jealousy and the like, which in turn are manifested in a variety of behaviours. In each single case it is necessary to study the kinds of physical or psychological stimuli that provoke the psychologically hypersensitive reactions, how these are manifested, in which domains, and with which intensity.

Each psychotherpeutic process in this study consisted of such a search for areas of emotional hypersensitivity, and just as in the allergological studies, the patients' own observations and recordings constituted the most important data. Most of the data thus came from narratives noted during the psychotherapeutic sessions and from the patients' own recordings outside the sessions. This information was supplemented by Marcel Proust's novels and correspondence, and by the Danish writer Carsten Jensen's essays. Both writers were asthmatic and both have described the

---

[5] There have been several controversies in Denmark between patients who are convinced that they are allergic to certain types of food, and doctors who do not find any allergic tendencies when they subject these patients to allergological tests, see for example Mirdal (1992).

psychological and social implications of having a chronic illness, especially breathing difficulties.

Pathways of psychosomatic interactions: Premenstrual asthma as an example

I shall here use the interrelation between menstruation and asthma as an example of hypersensitivity at the different levels of this psychosomatic spiral. Clinical evidence as well as research findings suggest that some women with asthma experience an exacerbation of their symptoms in the premenstrual period and the first days of menstruation. The term premenstrual asthma has been used to define the worsening of asthma symptoms and pulmonary function in relation to menstruation. Asthma seems to worsen at menstruation in about one-third of female patients, while it improves or is unchanged in others. Dalton (1964), Southam and Gonzaga (1965), and Hanley (1981), Smolensky, Reinberg, Lee and McGovern (1974) and Eliasson et al. (1987). These studies have, however, focused only on **physiological** processes in relation to premenstrual asthma and have not taken into consideration the **emotional and cognitive** status of the subjects, their individual vulnerabilities, personality dispositions and social conditions, even though these psychosocial factors are of relevance both on their own account and because they play an important role for the hormones that influence both menstruation and respiration.

I therefore proposed to investigate whether psychological factors affect bronchial hyperreactivity in those asthma patients who experience an exacerbation of their symptoms around menstruation time, and if so, to elucidate the mechanisms through which the two forms of hyperreactivity are related.

Five of the 10 women in the treatment group reported changes in asthma symptoms around menstruation time; four reported worsening of symptoms and one an improvement; there was no noticeable relation between asthma and menstruation in the remaining women. As to emotional changes around the time of menstruation, eight of the 10 women reported increased levels of irritability, tension and tearfulness, tiredness and restlessness, as well as occasional aggressive overreaction to conflicts and daily hustles. These symptoms, which correspond to the above-mentioned definition of psychological hyperreactivity, can be illustrated by the following case.

One of the subjects, a 20-year-old waitress, works at a restaurant which is well known for its friendliness toward families with young children. She likes children, and took this job because the restaurant was informal and children could run freely around the place. "But every now and then", she said, "I can become extremely irritated by those kids, and I even yell at them, and then I invariably know that I am going to have my period." A daily diary and visual analogue scale with respect to changes of mood confirmed the subjective feeling of heightened hyperreactivity around menstruation. This subject has been repeatedly hospitalized for asthma attacks, which she attributed to infections until her mother remarked that they always occurred in connection with menstruation.

It is important to note that there were variations in the occurrence and intensity of perimenstrual symptoms (both physical and emotional) from woman to woman, and in the same woman from period to period.

The frequency of about 4/10 in exacerbation of asthma around menstruation which was found in this study is in accordance with the published results on the prevalence of premenstrual asthma in the medical literature. The number of subjects in the present study is too low to warrant any generalization from these figures, but the results suggest that a considerable number of asthma patients may experience a worsening of their asthma around the premenstrual period, a fact which should be taken into consideration in the medical treatment and control of medication around these periods.

The results presented so far indicate an interrelationship between menstruation, exacerbation of asthma, psychological hyperreactivity and infections as background phenomena for premenstrual asthma. Once this interrelationship has been brought to evidence, the next step is to spell out the routes through which these factors might interact and affect the course of asthma. The present data suggest the following possible modes of interrelation:

1) A lowered resistance to infections in the premenstrual period→ exacerbation of asthma. Three of the four women who reported exacerbation of symptoms had repeated infections (colds, sinusitis, virus infections, bronchitis, influenza and gastrointestinal inflammation) in the premenstrual period. This is in line with earlier findings regarding the more frequent onset of various illnesses in the premenstrual phase than at any other time in the cycle (23).

2) A lowered resistance to stress → increased emotional hyperreactivity in the premenstrual period and first days of menstruation → exacerbation of asthma. Numerous studies have been made of premenstrual mood changes and behavioral symptoms in the psychiatric and psychological literature. As mentioned above, eight of the 10 women who participated in our study reported symptoms of stress and psychological hyperreactivity around the time of menstruation: They were more irritable, tired, depressed, self-depreciating and tense, and they reported that they were more affected by daily events and hustles that normally did not affect them as much[6].

The question of interest for this study was whether these psychological symptoms affected asthma, and if so, how. Not all women who had premenstrual distress experienced an exacerbation of asthma, but all those who reported an aggravation of their asthma around menstruation experienced also premenstrual distress. In other words, of the eight women who reported symptoms of psychological hyperreactivity at the paramenstruum, four experienced episodes of exacerbation of asthma around menstruation, whereas the other four, who also had psychological symptoms, experienced no exacerbation of asthma.

The data do not seem to indicate that differences in severity of premenstrual symptoms have played a role in this difference. It is, however, possible that more systematic data collection and rigorous use of, for example, the new diagnostic criteria for premenstrual distress, might yield other results.

3) An interactive effect between lowered resistance to stress, increased emotional hyperreactivity in the premenstrual period and first days of menstruation, lowered resistance to infections leading to the exacerbation of asthma. Psychological hypersensitivity and hyperreactivity during the premenstrual period does thus not necessarily and automatically lead to premenstrual asthma in all women, but it seems to constitute a risk factor

---

[6] This kind of evidence must of course be analyzed with caution. Changes of mood and discomfort are more liable to be attributed to premenstrual distress if they occur around the time of menstruation, whereas the same symptoms are attributed to other causes at other times. Furthermore, awareness of participating in a menstrual cycle study could be thought to increase the reporting of symptoms. (Recent data on this problem suggest, however, that this is not the case and that awareness of the focus of such a study does not significantly raise symptom reporting in previously asymptomatic women (Gallant et al, 1992)).

for certain asthma patients which, coupled with other "triggers", might precipitate an asthma attack.

An example of such a trigger in the present study was the lower resistance to infections. No causal relationship is implied in this hypothesis: the psychological alterations described above could be primary or secondary to the inflammatory processes. These phenomena are in fact so interrelated that it is not possible to disentangle cause from effect with our present methods. The results do, however, suggest that more attention should be paid to the period of menstruation in the clinical treatment of asthma. Some women might experience exacerbation of symptoms without being able to relate them to the psychological and immunological alterations around menstruation. In some cases, calling the patients' attention to this fact, and suggesting changes in therapeutic regimen and helping them to prevent and/or manage psychological stress as well as possible infections around the time of menstruation, might have beneficial consequences in the treatment of asthma.

"Concluding unscientific postscript"

At the beginning of this article, I described the psychosomatic spiral as a convenient model for delineating the complex interrelationship between biological, psychological and social processes in the human organism. The assumption was that changes at the physiological level, e.g., the onset of an asthma attack, would affect all the superior levels of the spiral; posture, muscular tonus, arousal, attention, concentration, cognitive functions, mood, irritability, motivation, social interactions, etc. Reciprocally, I also assumed that social and psychological factors at the higher levels of the spiral could provoke disregulation of all the underlying functions of the organism, including breathing.

Whereas the first part of the hypothesis, namely the disregulating effect of asthma on the psychological and social functions, was supported by the data, the second part of the hypothesis, namely the effects of the psychological factors on breathing, turned out to be much more difficult to assess. The difficulty lay mainly in the selection and prediction of the relevant "psychological factors" to be studied. The very meticulous analysis of the qualitative data suggests that seemingly unimportant events can provoke cognitive-emotional reactions that have far more profound consequences than apparently important life events and serious occurrences in a person's life. An expression of disapproval on a lover's face can in some instances be just as disruptive for good control of asthma as the movement of a seagull's wing can be the coincidental start of a chain reaction that ultimately provokes a tempest. The book "Åndenød", parts of which I have presented in this summary, was written in an attempt to illustrate the network of pathways through which thoughts and emotions may affect physiological functions.

I have attempted to show how these paths between "body and mind", which have so often been considered as two-directional, should rather be conceived as multidirectional and interrelated through open, permeable systems. In other words, we are not dealing with more or less distinct psychological and physiological systems, but with interwoven psyche-soma-spirals in constant movement. The very conception of physical and mental disorders as distinct categories seems no longer tenable in the face of such complexity.

References

Alexander, F., French, T.M. & Pollock, G.H. *Psychosomatic specificity*, vol. 1. Chicago: University of Chicago Press, 1968.
Als, H. Social interaction: dynamic matrix for developing behavioral organization. *Social interaction and communication in infancy. New Directions in Child Development*, vol 4, San Fransisco: Jossey Bass, 1979, 21-41.
Dalton, K. The influence of menstruation on health and disease. *Proceedings of the Royal Society of Medicine*, 1964, 57, 18-20.
Eliasson, O., Densmore, M.J., Scherzer, H.H. & Degraff, A.C. The effect of sodium meclofenamate in premenstrual asthma: A controlled clinical trial. *Journal of Allergy and Clinical Immunology*, 1987, 79, 909-918.
Gallant, S.J., Popiel, D.A. Hoffman, D.M., Chakraborty, P.K. Hamilton, J.A. Using daily ratings to confirm premenstrual syndrome/Late Luteal Phase Dysphoric Disorder. Part I. Effects of demand characteristics and expectations. *Psychosomatic Medicin*, 1992, 54, 149-166.
Hanley, S.P. Asthma variation with menstruation. *Br.J.Dis.Chest*, 1981, 75:306-308.
McDougall, J. *Le théatre du je*. Paris: Gallimard, 1984.
Minuchin, S., Rosman, B.L. & Baker, L. *Psychosomatic families*. Cambridge: Harvard University Press, 1978.
Mirdal, G.M. Mistro og allergi. Politiken, 23.11.1992.
Mirdal, G.M. *Åndenød. Astma i psykosomatisk perspektiv*. Kbh.: Munksgaard/Rosinante, 1994.
Shand, A.F. *The foundations of character*. London: MacMillan, 1920.

Smolensky, M.H., Reinberg, A., Lee, R.E. & McGovern, J.P. Secondary rhythms related to hormonal changes in the menstrual cycle: Special reference to allergology. In: M.Frein et al. (eds), *Biorhythms and human reproduction*. N.Y.: Wiley, 1974.

Southham, A. & Gonzaga, F.P. Systemic changes during the menstrual cycle. *American Journal of Obstetrics and Gynecology*, 1965, 91, 142-165.

Taylor, G.J. *Psychosomatic medicine and contemporary psychoanalysis*. Conn.: International University Press, 1987.

Weeke, B. Medicinsk-allergiske sygdomme. I: J. Welner, N. Reisby, V. Lunn & F. Schulsinger (eds.), *Psykiatri. En tekstbog*. Kbh.: FADL, 1985.

Weiner, H. *Psychobiology and human disease*. N.Y.: Elsevier, 1977.

Wilson, C.P. Family Psychopathology. I: C.P. Wilson & I.L. Mintz (eds.), *Psychosomatic symptoms: Psychodynamic treatment of the underlying personality disorder*. New Jersey: Jason Aronson Inc., 1989.

Young adults
Problems and research perspectives

SVEN MØRCH

Youth in a modern world

Youth life in all its dimensions has obviously become an issue which is more and more in focus. Young people themselves have become spectacular in new and provocative ways. Youth occupies a growing part of everyday life and attention. The focus on youth in public, political and scientific contexts, however, should be seen not only as a consequence of the visibility of youth or fears of and insecurity about new youth activities, but perhaps more as a consequence of the growing understanding of the significance of youth life in society.

The generally accepted picture of youth life today is that it is a period of individualisation or identity development, a time that should make young people able to cope with the adult world. It also seems to be generally understood that modern life has become difficult, demanding and complex, and that this makes youth development difficult or even a serious challenge for the individual.

Therefore, the characteristics of adult life and its demands on modern individualisation are of the greatest importance for the conceptualisation of youth life and our understanding of the challenges and possibilities of modern youth.

Youth life in itself has become so important that the attention on youth may have shifted from the "frame" to the "content", from youth time to youth life . But, although youth life is important, it is still necessary to remember that youth is "framed" by childhood and adult life. Young people still become adults in two ways: On the one hand, when they become responsible for children and perhaps marry, and on the other, when they have work and "make their own money". *To understand modern youth we have to look both at the process of individualisation and at the possibilities and problems involved in becoming an adult in modern society.*

Modern individualisation

When we look at some of the specifics of modern life, these appear in contrast to a – perhaps over-simplified – picture of a lost world.

Post-modernistic or late-modernistic theory points to highly complicated, demanding perspectives of individual development. In the spirit of Giddens' works (Giddens 1987, 1991) we might draw this picture:

From: Traditional society	**To: Modern society**
Find one's place in time and space: Learn social rules	Live across time and space: Develop self-identity
Have trust in expertise and authorities: Develop faith in authorities	Use different authorities and types of expertise: Develop reflexivity and self-assurance
Handle conflicts: Learn basic social norms, skills and interests	Handle conflicts: Develop social practice and contextual knowledge
Have trust in everyday life: Live within traditions and qualifications	Integrate in everyday life: Develop individual competences and ontological security

This general picture of modern individualisation shows that individuals today live in an open world. They move around and should develop some sort of self-understanding so that they are able to reflect and become discursive about themselves, others and the way people refer to each other in a changing society. But it also shows the dangers of not being able to cope with the world. Individuals today are in danger of losing their identities and their trust in themselves. They are individually and socially at risk.

Insofar as youth life of today is often described as increasingly complicated and demanding, this description may point to some of the demands which follow from the changes in individualisation. The question, however, does not seem to be whether youth life has become more demanding. *The question seems to be how far modern youth life fulfils the new demands on it, and what sorts of problems become important in this new situation.*

If we focus on individualisation in youth, a first picture of modern youth life may point to the following perspectives:

Because of the "function" of youth life as the period of life when young people develop into "modern individualistic society", youth life of today has become increasingly central to the individual's development. These new demands on individualisation seem to have prolonged youth life, perhaps to such a degree that youth development "bursts its boundaries" to fulfil its "function". Not only do young people become youths earlier in their lives, but youth life is prolonged as well. This prolongation creates new youth life styles and perspectives, as can be seen, for example, in the concept of "young adults".

Our first observation might be that individuals today become youths very early, but adults very late, and the difficulties of becoming adults make the situation of "young adults" a modern reality. But to become a young adult is perhaps a very ambiguous situation: It creates the possibility for youngsters to stay young but at the same time it stops them from becoming adults.

Young adults as a construct or a reality

If we look at modern or "late-modern" life and learn from modernistic theory at the same time, one of the first lessons of modernization seems to be that the social world is constructed, and *concepts are the building stones of this construction*. "Young adults" is one of these new concepts. By inventing and using the concept "young adults", we construct and reconstruct the social world in the same conceptual movement: Life becomes more complex, it does not only consist of children, youth and adults. "Young adults" has forced itself into our attention by what may be nothing more than a simple conceptual trick.

The first challenge in analysing the new concept and reality of young adults is to clarify the perspectives of this constructivist approach to social reality. The question seems to be whether or not young adults only exist as a new and sociological concept. Does some reality exist behind the concept? And if so, what does it look like and how do we describe or analyse it?

To demonstrate that the concept of "young adults" does not only point to some ideological construction, we might consider the different possibilities which exist for the use of the concept. Young adults may be understood in several ways or at several levels. The following small diagrams show some of these different levels. If we start with the "construction of the phenomenon" the picture looks like this:

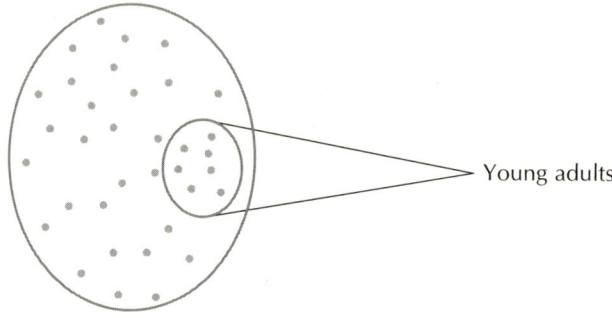

Fig. 1. Young adults as an individual and visible phenomenon in a population

Firstly, the concept of young adults might point to specific individuals and individual ages (20 to 30) (fig.1). Young people may become visible as young adults because of individual qualities in their persons which are identified by the concept. Individual qualities may be not only age, but ways of behaviour in its broad sense. We think that we know what we are talking about when we point to a young person and use the concept of young adult.

Secondly, the concept may point to young adults as a social construction experienced by the subjects themselves (fig 2). Young adults become able to think of themselves within the concept. "I feel I am a young adult". Youngadults may be a subjective reality.

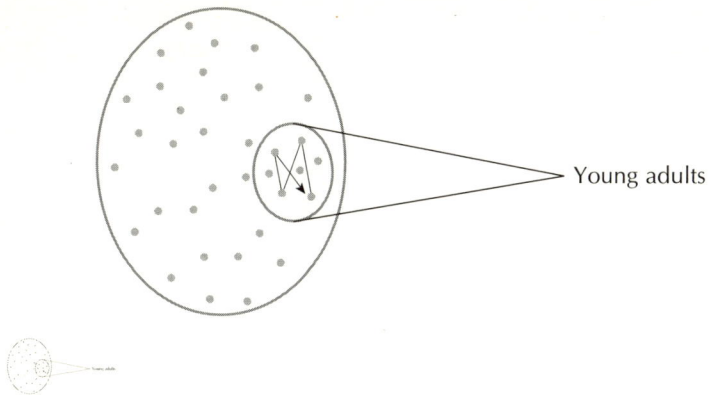

Fig. 2. Young adults as a subjective reality

Thirdly, the concept may point to young adults as an objective reality, meaning that young adults can be seen as a broad existing social phenomenon, which might be understood as a social category made possible or created by social conditions (fig 3). Young adults exist as a reality in social life. Young adults may do something, or their activities may make a difference.

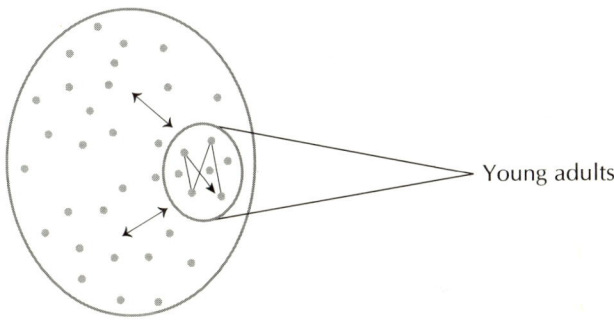

Fig. 3. Young adults as an objective reality

Fourthly, the concept may point to this social category not only as a visible and existing phenomenon, but as a phenomenon with a social history, as a developed phenomenon.

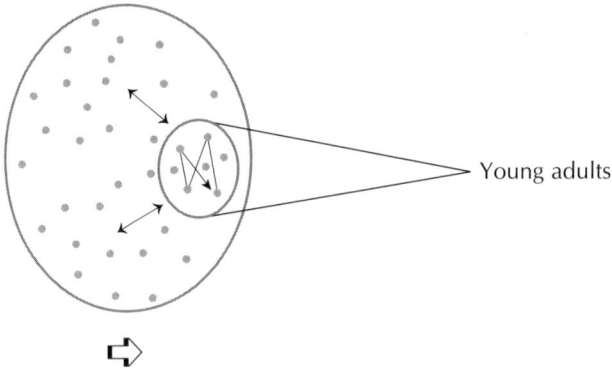

Fig. 4. Young adults as a historical construction

These different levels point to different aspects and interests in the use of the concept and in the use of a social constructionist perspective.

In the discussion on young adults, however, these levels often become confused, making discussion and clarification difficult. For example, most statistical information is only able to tell the history of individual young adults from the perspective of individual age, but is used to describe a specific young adult phenomenon. Descriptions of new lifestyles do not tell of the specific young adult situation or of how young adults "master youth life ". Lifestyle becomes simply "cultural activities" of the age group, but is mostly seen as "defining" the phenomenon. For this reason we very often find ourselves lacking sufficient information to widen our knowledge of young adults as a social and cultural phenomenon.

Levels of analysis – or how should reality be analysed?
If we leave this discussion of young adult concepts and turn to an analytical position, it becomes obvious that young adults should be analysed as a new reality; and that several options to the study of reality exist. We may look at reality in a direct or descriptive way, from a theoretical perspective, from different social and political positions, from a historical perspective, etc.

If we want analytically to unfold our understanding of a new phenomenon as "young adults" one possibility is to "go backwards" within the small models of the constructional levels of young adults. One way of analysing this new reality of youth could be to find out why and how the phenomenon developed as a historical construction, and what consequences this development has for youth life style development and on individual lives. To do so, we might ask questions in another way. Firstly , we should understand the lifestyle of young adults as a historical construction, a historically developed lifestyle (fig 4) Secondly, we might understand young adults as a social category, a basic youth life condition, to be formed in social groups and among individuals (fig 3). Thirdly, we might look at young adults as a cultural lifestyle, a subjective and meaningful way of life (fig 2) And fourthly, we could see it as an individual developmental possibility, a possibility of living as a young adult (fig 1).

This way of analysing youth life and young adults looks at individual activities as activities of youth life made possible and actualised in modern societal development. This understanding is also built on a general theory of social activity. To unfold these perspectives we may draw a broader picture of activity theory.

Elements of an activity youth theory
Human activity is intentional activity in mastering tasks or challenges. The basics of an activity perspective might be shown in this model:

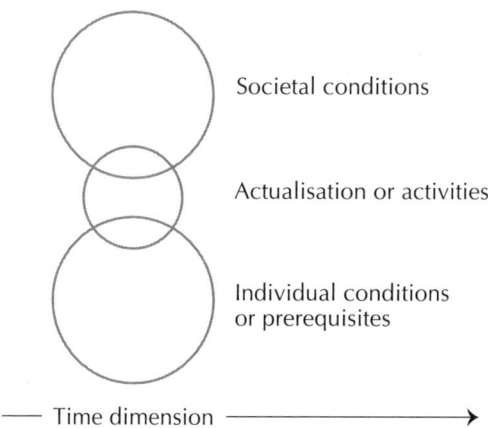

Fig. 5. Activities as actualisation

The model illustrates a widely accepted tenet of activity theory: When the individual does something, he actualises conditions in a specific situation or social context.

On the one hand, he uses societal conditions or acts within conditions as possibilities and constraints of action. The individual actualises conditions in activity. Conditions as historically developed possibilities and constraints of human activity are often contradictory and diffuse. They are, however, the rules and resources of the situation. For this reason the individual both uses and changes societal conditions in his activity. Societal conditions exist in social contexts, they organise social contexts, for example in the case of the school system and school curriculum. School as a social context of youth in this way exhibits the possibilities and constraints of youth life , but at the same time youth is part of the process of changing the school.

On the other hand, the individual uses his own previous experiences and personal capacities as his individual conditions of action. In actualisation, the individual uses himself in his societal activity. He actualises his own potentialities in the situation and according to the conditions of the situation. Through this process, he develops himself and further capacities.

In actualisation, the individual's understanding of both societal and individual conditions plays a central role.[1] To the individual, different aspects of both societal and individual conditions seem important or meaningful. The particular conditions the individual finds important in the specific situation are crucial to the mastering of actual problems or tasks, and the conditions the individual finds important in understanding his or her own life are important to the development of individual self-understanding. The development of this self-understanding takes place in the social relationship in the context. Social relations and interaction become crucial in actualisation.

To illustrate individual activity as part of social life, the picture of activity might be expanded in this way (fig. 6, next page):

---

[1] The importance of individual understanding of social conditions in individual activity is stressed in Critical Psychology. (Holzkamp, K. 1983, Tolman, C.W & W Maiers 1991, Dreier, O. 1993)

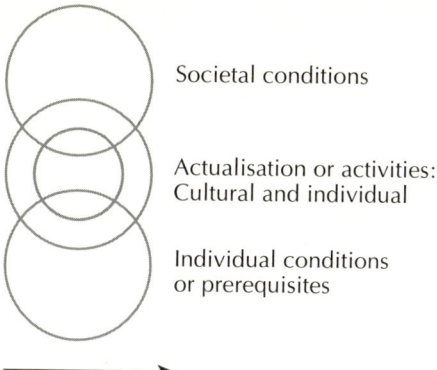

Fig. 6. Activities as social actualisation

The model now shows that actualisation exists not only as an individual activity, but that the individual is part of a social category or a social group. Actualisation and forms of actualisation develop within social relations. The actualisation of societal conditions is the project of more involved individuals, and forms of mastering or actualisation exist in the social context. They are developed forms of activities according to the understanding of possibilities and constraints of social life. Youth cultures, for example, should be seen as such forms of meaningful activity patterns. *Youth cultures are activities made by youngsters in mastering youth life.* Individuals learn from each other, they interact and develop new forms of activities to overcome and solve contradictions in societal conditions.

At the same time, individuals develop activities by the use of individual preconditions, and individuals often share individual conditions. Although individual conditions belong to the individual, they may be more or less the same for several individuals. The development of forms of actualisation, then, should not only be seen as determined by societal conditions. Shared individual conditions, however, do not determine forms of actualisation in a simple way. Individual conditions should be seen as tools or means of actualisation and their influence should be seen in this respect.

The activity theory model now points to further conclusions. Individuals act within social contexts. In doing so, they share and develop experiences of social action, so individuals and society should not be seen as contradictory. Contradictions exist mainly within or among societal conditions or within individual conditions, not between the individual and societal levels in a general way. Societal conditions and individual conditions are the tools of actualisation, and even though they sometimes seem far from each other, they are the rules and resources of actualisation.

In actualisation, individuals develop both societal and individual conditions. The acts of the individual should be seen as ways of mastering conditions and contradictions in his life within a social group, which at the same time changes and develops its own conditions.

To complete the activity theoretical model for the analysis of youth it should be drawn like this:

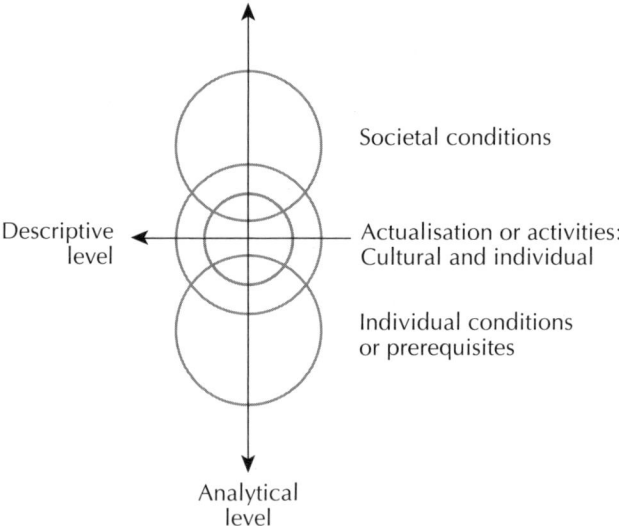

Fig. 7. *Analytical levels in activity theories.*

As the model shows, youth activities may be *described* at the level of individual and cultural activities. At this level, what youngsters do both individually and together becomes *visible*.

But the problem with making theories or analysis at this *descriptive level* is that young people's activities are not necessarily seen as youth activities. They are only visible as individual or group phenomena. Yet the observer may feel free to understand and explain individual activities from his own perspective. Youth activities or behaviour may be "explained" as marginality problems, identity problems, drug problems, prostitution, etc., or they may be "understood" or interpreted as normative or culturally symbolic phenomena All of these perspectives may catch important aspects of youth life and development, but they do not see the problems as integral parts of youth life in its broad sense. Only by accepting the overall *analytical* position or dimension of the model does the social scientist or any other bystander become aware of the necessity of understanding or explaining youth activities and problems as the ways *young people develop youth life in their active mastering of youth conditions by individual engagement*.

How to analyse young adults

If we should sum up the consequences of this thinking according to the analysis of young adults, we may go back to figures 1-4 and look at the constructionist perspectives of young adults, but from the analytical level: It is necessary to analyse youth development as a historical construction: The ways in which youth life is constructed and the consequences for young people's individualization. As an objective reality today: How conditions are organised in youth development as rules and resources of the individualization process. As a subjective reality: The ways in which young people use youth life in organising social activities and themselves. And as an individual phenomenon: The ways in which individual uses and reorganises his own past experiences in his or her participation in youth life.

Youth life as change: a general frame of reference

Our first observation, that individuals today become youths very early but adults very late, pointed to the contradictory situation of youth: The prolongation of youth life as a development possibility and as a restriction on the responsibility of adult life. To understand this new situation which perhaps "creates young adults", youth life development should be considered as a social and individual construction.

Youth activity, and the phenomenon of youth itself, develops within organised and organising conditions of youth life. In actualising youth conditions, individuals create youth life and youth. Youth life becomes part of the individualization of modern society and youth becomes a building block of individualization in history. To find out about youth life content and its organisation, we may learn from a short glimpse at history.

Youth life developed within the development of bourgeois society – at the end of the eighteenth century – as a condition of individual development from child to adult in accordance with the separation of family and work. On the one hand, the development of a "private" family made the child central to the family and provided specific conditions for "childish" development, which made it necessary to change the child into a adult. On the other hand, the development of working life, the development of technical and organisational structures which demanded a high level of skills and competence. not only in the work situation but in the broader political and organisational life, made a youth and school life necessary.

Youth as we see it is a developmental phase and an individual quality developed by a specific youth life in a school system. Youth life was expected to change and develop the child, to enable it to take part in bourgeois working and political life. Children had to become individuals in the "modern" changing society, and this meant that they "left" the dependent child status of family life. They had to develop technical and practical competence (qualifications for the new societal influence of the bourgeoisie class) and they also had to develop social competence for these new positions. As an overall concept of the goal of youth development, which includes both technical qualifications and individual and social competence, we may talk about *youth individualization as a development of qualified self-determination*.

Although youth life today exists as a developmental condition for most children, this is a result of a long history. It took many years before youth developed in different groups and parts of society. When it happened it seems to have been the result of a necessity for "individualization" and for this reason "to have youth" in most social groups e.g. girls, middle class, farmers and working class.[2] When youth developed, however, it developed as a time frame possibility for adult development *within* the specific social group or social class to which the individual belonged. Youth became a "necessary" *developmental phase according to the specific demands of adult life* as they existed within different social groups or social classes.[3]

The development of youth as a "class version" of youth life might be shown as in this very general model:

---

[2] The development of youth among girls is always late. Youth is a construction of qualification for work. As long as women are kept away from equal job possibilities, youth development is slow. The Oxford dictionary says, that youth means a young man; all young people everywhere at all times; or the state or period of life of being young. According to this dictionarey it can not refer to a girl.

[3] For a broader description of this development see Mørch, S. (94). The work of Hollingshead, A.B. (1949) and later the Birmingham school (e.g. Cohen. P. 1972 and Clarke, J. et al. 1976) also illustrate youth development as a class phenomenon.

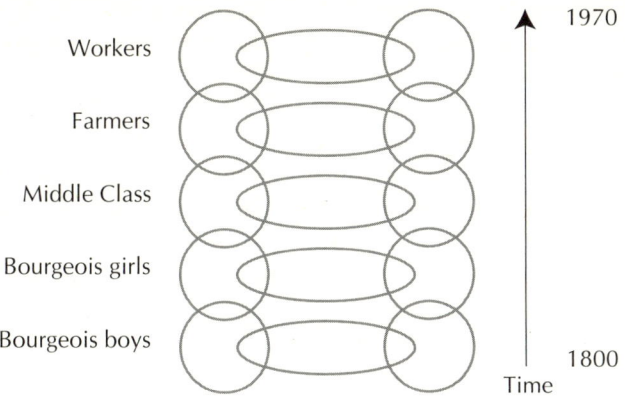

Fig. 8. The development of youth-life

The point of the model is that although youth life develops in different social groups and social classes, it does not mean that youth life becomes the same for all youth. In stratified societies youth develops as a stratified individualization and not as a means of social mobility Youth life developed as the individualization period of the specific social group. Its frame and content developed according to the adult conditions of the specific group or class.

The challenge of modern youth
The most general and fundamental change of modern, and perhaps especially Scandinavian, youth life is that it has become the central means or agent of social mobility.

Youth life today no longer changes the child into a adult within the social group or class. Youth life today is *the period of societal individualization* in a new sense, an individualization according to new social positions. Today youth life both moves the youngster from childhood into adult life, and moves the youngster away from his family social position into new social positions. Youth life individualization has become the principal institution of modern social mobility: Individualization for a society based on educational qualifications.

Since the sixties, Danish youth life has become common and more or less the same for all youngsters. Life in school and pedagogical institutions has become a normal or general condition of child and youth development The Danish school system in particular has been the organiser of a general youth period which is more or less the same for all youngsters.

School developed its new goals as "equality through education". This means that most youngsters, both boys and girls, were offered the same conditions of youth life and for this reason, in principle the same opportunities in work and adult life. This development is perhaps not the cause, but it is a central condition of modern youth life . It shows that societal individualization has become the main task of school life at the same time as school life has become "the same" for most youngsters. Youth life has become not only the time of "growing up", but the time of social change.

The significance of youth life has changed in this process. When most youth experience the same conditions of youth life, they are given equal conditions of adult life. The significance of modern Scandinavian youth life may be shown like this:

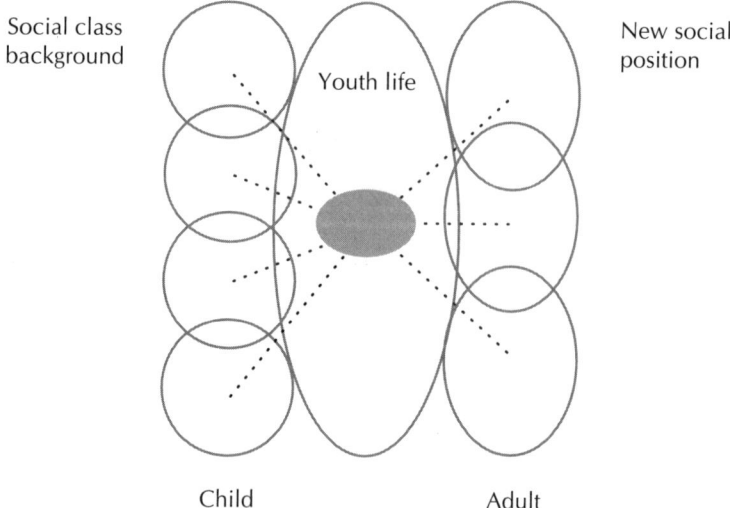

Fig 9. The modern youth challenge

The figure shows the "transforming" character of youth life at the individual level, and at the same time points to the general contemporary change of modern "class society" to a less class-based organisation of different income groups. As this model shows, the period of youth has become not only an "individual transformer" changing children to adults, but a "social transformer" too: By use of the youth period the individual may be able to change his or her social position. Youth life has become the central means of social mobility.

The consequences of the creation of this "new youth life" are extensive Firstly, young people today have become less dependent on social background and family conditions. The making of the future is their own responsibility. Secondly, youth life becomes important for an individual's adult social position.

In this way, youth life becomes much more important to youth. The way they engage and cope with youth conditions becomes crucial for their future social position and adult life. Youth life has become the phase of societal individualization in a new sense. Youngsters have to create their own social position through individual engagement in youth life. For this reason youth life has become the central challenge in individual development. Youth success or failure has become part of youth life. Youth life engagement decides youth future much more then ever before.

This picture of youth is now part of a common-sense understanding which may be easily illustrated: Thirty years ago, when a girl invited her new boyfriend home, her parents asked him about his father's occupation.

Today they ask the boyfriend about his own education or engagement in youth life. The interest is the same, only the question has changed.

Modern youth life has also become "stressed". Individual success or failure seems to follow from individual activities. This situation makes youth life a problem for the individual. It causes youth problems Obviously, the individual needs greater support to manage this situation, or perhaps he or she needs a prolongation of youth life, which not only gives the individual more time, but supports individual development by offering a "new" structure of individual development. Before, youth life was part of a social class society, which made youth life "secure" for those who had one. Perhaps the new, prolonged youth life offers a new security in educational society: The security of belonging to the educational group. Perhaps the modern life of "young adults" as a prolongation of youth life should be seen from this position. It both helps individual development in a modern educational society, and helps reestablish a social structure for individual development.

The problem in this situation seems to be: What happens to the group of youngsters who do not belong to the new "educational youth"?

Youth life today

Without going into further analysis of the history of youth development, it is possible to draw an overall picture of youth life today. Youth conditions today exist within social arenas or social contexts. This model shows the principal organisation of modern youth life.

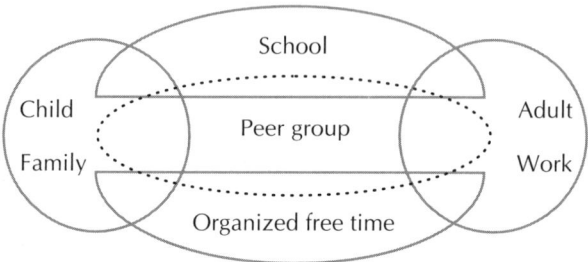

Fig 10. Modern youth-life

In the development of youth life, school life is still fundamental. But today several institutional settings organise conditions of competence or qualifications for adult life.

Child school (e.g. primary school[4]) and youth school were originally separated in different institutions. Today, this has changed Danish children, for example, go to the same school from first to tenth grade and the school develops the difference between children and youth within its curriculum by the way the teachers treat the children/youngsters. To be a child or a youth has become a contextual social construction defined and redefined in the situation. School life organises the development of its pupils according to the curriculum of the school which is built up as "the way to become an adult" in contemporary society. In this way school organises developmental conditions for the development of qualified self-determination.

As more and more children were kept in school, leisure time developed From the beginning of this century leisure time became the interest of

---

[4] This distinction is too simple. At the end of the eighteenth century the school system for the broad population was not only short, but not age-aware. It was mostly a school system for the teaching of religion and morals. (See Aries 1973, Nelleman 1966)).

several political and pedagogical interventions. Youth time should be organised to develop children or to prevent youth making problems. Today most youngsters in Denmark use "youth-clubs" for a period of their lives.

Scout movements, sports and pedagogical work all offer conditions for youth life. Historically, these organised parts of youth life have focused the social development of youth. In recent years the goals of individual social development have especially been democratic social participation.

In Denmark, since the end of the fifties the youth group or peer group has become more influential. The peer group came into existence as youth life became accepted by adults and the young people themselves. Youth had to become a normal phenomenon to make a "free" youth life acceptable. However, as described in several places, the peer group today is gaining in influence in the lives of young people. In the peer group, the youngsters may learn forms of activity for mastering youth life and they learn to co-operate and become part of a social group.

The overall picture of youth today is that youth life conditions exist as possibilities for all youngsters. However, youth life as actualisation of youth conditions varies. Youth life today is open to all, but it is actualised in different ways by different youth groups.

Problems and changes of youth life

Until this point, I have tried to describe youth life in its basic construction and development. Youth life, however, is not only harmonious. Youth life contains contradictions, which cause youth life to vary and become a serious challenge to youth. Youth life contradictions also create varied youth life actualisations and in this way make *youth life change*.

Youth life as a time of societal individualization and as a transformer between family and work life is sensitive to modern developments The more family life and work life become separated in time and space expectations of human functions, the more difficult the change from child to adult becomes. No other period in history or in individual human life demands such a change of personality as that which we see today. Youth life in itself has become a challenge. The extension of youth life seems reasonable just from this fact. Youth life prolongation seems reasonably for making personality change and development possible. To become qualified for the modern world, more and more youngsters are placed in educational systems for longer and longer period of their lives For this reason they stay young, or they are defined as young people in terms of adult occupations. They are partly youth and partly adults. *They become "young adults"*:

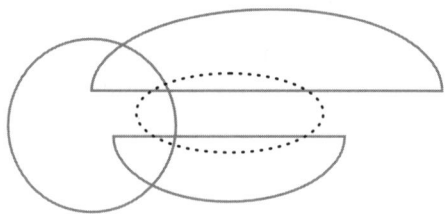

Fig. 11. Educational youth prolongation

Naturally, youth life as an organised, professional construction has changed in this process. The school and educational system has changed, developing its curriculum and pedagogical methods, and leisure time conditions have developed accordingly. The difficulties of youth life have become better supported, but the expectations of grown- up life become increasingly stronger, creating pressure in youth life. Youth life is in any case becoming more and more difficult for the individual to cope with, and demands on motivation, engagement and understanding of youth conditions become crucial for the individual's own development becomes crucial.

Contemporary youth life also contains other serious problems. Because of unemployment and restricted means of further education, youth life does not always look as we may expect. To many youngsters, no adult life possibilities seem open. They will have no further education and no job.

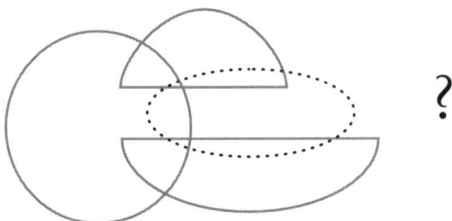

Fig. 12. Youth with short education and without future

To young people in this situation, engagement in organised youth life, in school and organised leisure time activities becomes difficult. It is difficult to see any perspectives or goals and for this reason engagement in youth conditions perhaps does not seem "worth the trouble" This explains the fact that for many youngsters, youth life is seen as an obstacle to adult development, so they leave school, education and pedagogical youth activities.

Perhaps their youth life centres around the peer group. Within the peer group, young people find a social life which they themselves may make meaningful, as may be shown in this model:

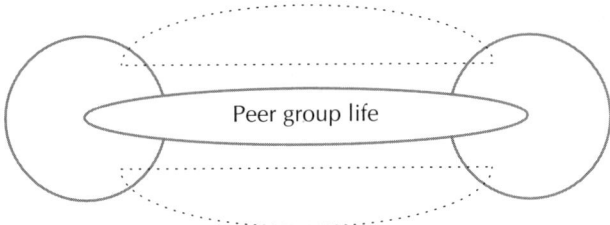

Fig. 13. The peer group youth

The peer-group may be important for youth social development, and often youth life and projects develop from this "modern" youth life But the youth peer group often develops into a problem situation. Young people do not use the developmental channels into the adult world. They feel expelled, and the peer group becomes the only road to adult life.

To many young people, not only does youth life cause problems, but they see no perspectives in adult life. Low-skilled or uneducated, they will experience problems in getting a job in the modern "educational world". They are kept young or as "young adults" in the sense of not being admitted to the adult world.

The "container youth" situation

The problem of offering further education and jobs to young people has caused a change in youth life as a societal, organised period of adult development. More and more young people leave school without any possibilitiesof further education or career directions. They become young unemployed. The official answer to this situation is the making of youth unemployment projects of various kinds. In this way a new youth life is created – "container youth", a place to put youngsters for whom no other possibilities exist:

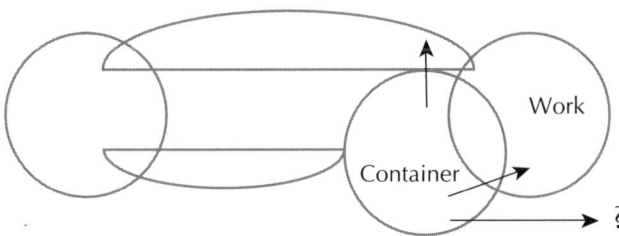

Fig. 14. Container youth development

The interesting perspective of this situation is, however, that "container youth life" contains youth with very different life perspectives. Although they are all seen as "unemployed", they themselves may have different perspectives on their lives. Some hope to return to education, some hope for work, and some have no adult work plans. Again, young people in this situation are being kept young or as "young adults" in the sense of not being admitted to the adult world.

Several varieties of youth life exist today. These diagrams, however, may be sufficient to show some of the basic problems of modern youth life. The diagrams also show that young adults are differentiated between "educational young adults" and "non-educational young adults".

The new youth or adult life: young adults

In understanding the development of young adults, the prolongation of youth life and social change become important. At the descriptive level we find that a growing proportion of young people in their twenties remain parked in the educational system or in "youth or unemployment projects". They are not part of adult working life and they are not responsible for family and children. Often they live a "single life" and have no children until the end of their twenties. They may be seen as having lots of possibilities, as being "free", or they may be seen as marginalised in society. This double view points to several ways in which young adults are presented in both popular, political and theoretical thinking.

Precisely for these reasons, interest may develop in questions such as; what they are doing, what they think about life and what perspectives they may have about society. Young adults exist, and from a scientific and political position it becomes interesting and perhaps necessary to know who they are and how they are, to know their "culture" and to know their political standpoint and if they seem to be becoming a problem of social integration. Youth life makes social science important.

In the discussion on young adults, the focus is most frequently on "educational youth". Young adults are defined as educational youth, and young adults may be seen as the result of prolonged education in a modern "educational world". If, however, we take a more theoretical perspective, some new ideas may develop and some new research perspectives may arise.

Youth life has obviously been both broadened and prolonged. The new demands of societal individualization put all youth competitors "on equal ground" and in this way "broaden" youth life. Youth life belongs to all, both as it is organised officially by the school and through leisure-time activities, and also as it is formed by consumer industries and professional youth media.

The challenges of "the complex society" and modern individualization also prolong youth. Young people spend more and more time in school and education in tough competition with each other, and a large proportion of youth find themselves in a waiting position; waiting for an education, or waiting for an adult job and acceptance. It seems that youth "broadening", or the democratic youth policies which make youth life the same for all, is both supplemented and opposed by youth prolongation. The lives of young adults are varied. In particular, we experience a difference between educational youth and non-educational youth.

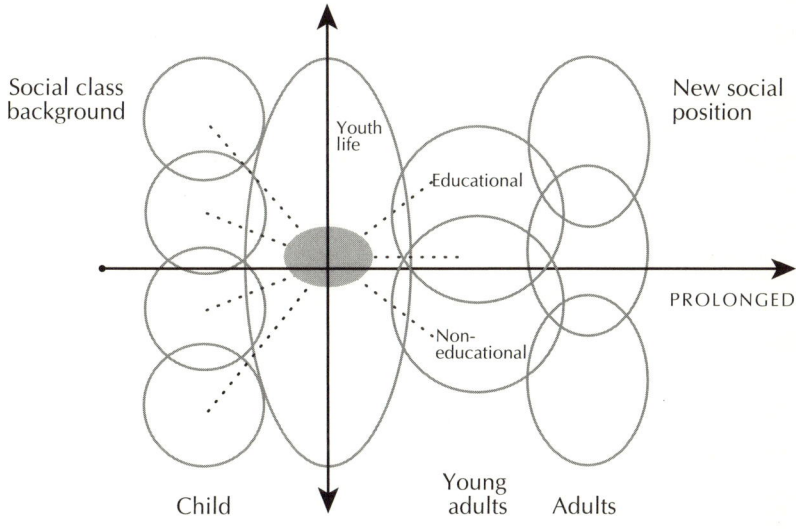

Fig. 15. Modern youth-life: broadened and prolonged

This model points to this new situation – youth life as broad and prolonged at the same time – but also to the fact that young adult life seems to be differentiated according to adult life organisation. It may seem as if young adult life develops "in between" the modern "equal" youth life and a still "unequal" adult life.

Our observation may be that youth life has been both broadened and prolonged, and that this situation seems to have differentiated young people within young adult life.

This new situation seems to parallel the situation of historical youth development itself. Youth developed as a bourgeois construction, and for this reason youth belonged to the bourgeois class. But it became the standard for other youngsters too. All young people came to be evaluated as more or less "young". The creation of youth created a non-youth at the same time as a negative picture of youth.[5] Youth developed a residual youth too.

The same situation seems to be developing today. Young adults are seen as "free" youngsters in the education system in a developmental situation. And though this situation contains serious problems, especially with regard to economy, it is different from the picture of the opposite situation, marginalised youth. Marginalised young people are not seen as young adults, but as "container youth" or problem youth. They are the residual youth in an educational society.

Young adults or adults
The picture of modern young adults should, however, be modified. The prolonged youth life does not necessarily apply to all groups in society. We still have youth development which follows a more "traditional picture of youth development". Even though more and more training for work today takes place in educational institutions, we still have some on-the-job training left. Some youngsters go directly from school to some sort of on-the-job training. Their situation should perhaps not be characterised as "youth" or "prolonged youth" at all, but as "adult youngsters".

This group is becoming smaller and smaller in modern society, but they still illustrate a trajectory in youth development, and also a consequent

---

[5] This should be understood in the way that the existence of youth as a concept and a social construction in the bourgeois class made it possible to see that children in lower classes were not real youth.

social middle group in society. They also still define the contours of the middle group in modern Scandinavian society.

Without making the picture too complex, we might say that the middle group in modern society has a double recruitment base, from the traditional training-situation and from modern educational youth.

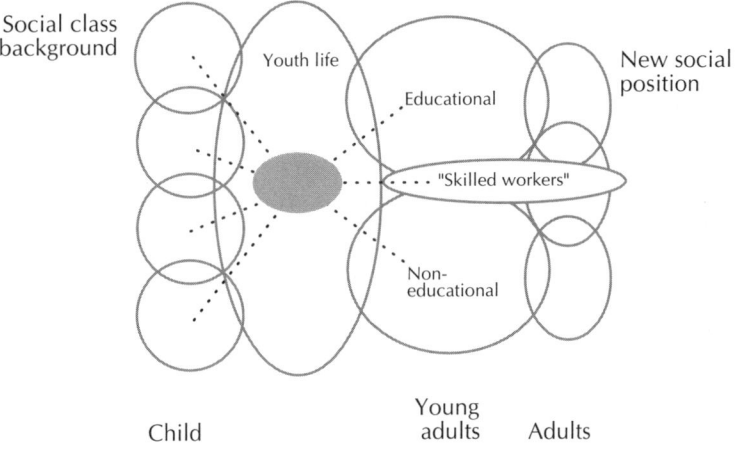

Fig. 16. Young adults as defined by grown-up society

The reason this situation is important is that it points to a specific change and contradiction in modern youth. Adult youngsters are in a totally different situation from young adults. They are defined and "constructed" as adults according to their work situation, even though they are perhaps not seen as "adults" in its broad sense.

The contradictions of young adult development

Youth theory has shown that youth for its construction is based on adult life, but for its actualisation or individual realisation it should be seen from the point of the individual to.

If we try to understand young adults as resulting from a prolonged youth period, the first questions point to an interest in understanding and focusing central issues in the "construction" of young adults both as an objective and a subjective new youth period.

The overall lesson from the analysis of youth life was that the youth life of today is the constructed time for societal individualization. This means that young people in their youth life have to look for their future interests and social position. The objective and subjective youth construction meet in youth actualisation or youth life. *Youth life looks for the structure and possibilities in adult life and in this respect youth life may be seen as the answer to adult life organisation.*

The basic structure of adult life has also changed. The basic change taking place in social life, both as it "exists" in some way, and as it is made possible in the education system, is *from* some sort of class system with different and acceptable positions *to* a more "democratic society". Various concepts have been used to describe this new social system: Middle class society, 2/3 society etc. The main point in all these descriptions, however, is, that modern society is a centralised and centralising society with individuals revolving around it. Modern society has more and more become a unifying society. We are all "members of society", and education has become the differentiating criterion in this world. The problem of winning and losing is not a social or societal problem, but an individual one. Social position is a possibility for the individual, not an unjust societal restriction or structural condition.

Education is directed mainly at certain social positions, and the reason youngsters engage in education is because they want some sort of position in society. So prolonged youth life is basically, as an educational life, part of the new individualization in society. Both the educational system and the individuals see society in this way.

The consequences of this perspective seem to be that young adult life is basically constructed around education, and for this reason it is a life period for modern society's successful individualization.

This situation creates several problems. Prolonged youth life, the life of young adults, is the life of young people who are broadly accepted as adults, but are still in the educational system. For this reason they are placed in a conflict situation. As adults they are expected and expect from themselves, to be able to influence their own life. But as pupils in educational systems they are considered as non-adults. And as youngsters in terms of education/jobs they are left without money and opportunities to do things which are regarded as obvious for adults. This situation may create criticism , protest and political commitment.

The double perspectives of young adults

This situation also causes differentiation in the life of young adults; the positive and the negative prolongation of youth life. On the one hand, young adults who are given very good opportunities in their lives develop young adult lifestyles, which easily magnify individualistic aspirations and behaviour. They may develop an understanding of themselves as some sort of super individuals who can change the world according to their own perspectives.

On the other hand, of course, the minus variant creates anxieties. Many young adults are not involved in "young adult life" as the basic educational life. They are kept outside the main development of modern "educational society". The consequence may be that they actively form alternative ways of life. They have been put at a side track, and most of the evidence shows that it is difficult to get back to the main track again.

This development of an alternative way of life may be necessary and important, but also it may create big problems. On the one hand, all youngsters of today are individualised, they are able to do things and they are mostly aware of personal interests and perspectives. Young adults in this "minus situation" may for this reason become "individualistic oppositionists". They may develop strategies for survival which disregard overall social perspectives. Societal individualization becomes anti-societal individualization if society does not create opportunities and conditions for development.

The telescope perspective
When young adult life is analysed as a new phase of societal individualization another perspective should also be focused upon.

Even though adult life, and the means for realisation of adult qualification exist as socially and societally distributed possibilities, youngsters are influenced to see and understand adult life in most confusing ways.

To many young people, young adult and adult life is pictured mainly in terms of the plus and minus variants of the individual's own ambitions, and perhaps initiative. The minus variant in particular is pictured as the result of individual failure. But the plus variant is also mainly seen as the result of individual ambitions and individual interest. The broad picture in society, of a unifying society open to individual variation, hides the driving forces of modern integration and differentiation. The media, especially, portray the "happy" individualistic life. Ordinary official and semi-official education and life perspectives often seem to be absent from media and other public pictures. Youth media in particular have become part of and creator of an especially fanciful youth picture. Not only do music and music groups seems to provide an individual opportunity, but "young adult leisure life" also appears as a new, general phenomenon.

The results may be seen as some sort of telescope perspective, both from the structural perspective and for the individual: To many young people, societal individualization is developed as if the plus variant, the success-perspective, is realistic for all, as if it is an individualistic result and is just close at hand, very easy to achieve. If young people just stretch out their hands they can touch the young adult success life.

The consequences of this picture and the individual telescope strategies should perhaps be focused upon much more in understanding the development of young adult life.

Research perspectives
If the perspective of societal individualization as a constitutional and actualised developmental possibility is clarified, more research perspectives develop.

Both the development of the broad "middle young adult life" and the gender differences in young adult life should be researched. How do young people live their lives within social conditions, how do they answer to the inherent contradictions between being young and adult at the same time? How does it influence education and how does it influence private life?

If, however, the focus is at the problem groups, we may develop research into the questions of how problem groups are created, and how young adults might change or develop their situation.

Immigrant youth in particular should be analysed in this frame. It seems necessary to find out what perspectives are open to immigrant youth in respect of young adult life. How do they manage their lives, and what are the consequences for immigrant youth of engaging in young adult life, for their future live and for their social and familial relations? What is the consequence for immigrant youth of engaging in young adult life?

This problem seems most central to the Danish questions of immigrant integration. Integration is seen as a necessary policy, but its means of achievement and consequences are still very much open to debate and development.

The research perspectives should also ask questions in terms of the general theoretical understanding and the specific situation.

In my view this new concept should be analysed from two perspectives. One is *the changes in society* which make this life-period come about and make it central to individual development. The other is *the change in youth life actualisation as the transformation between childhood and adult worlds.*

Changing youth life is a still ongoing process, from its development in the bourgeoisie at the end of the eighteenth century to its "popularisation" or "spreading" to all social classes after the second world war.

The changes in youth life seem to be "caused" by societal changes. Demands for qualifications and democratic development in society make individual development of a "qualified-self-determination" necessary. *Democratisation calls for a popularisation of youth life and industrialisation for a prolongation of school life in different social groups.* This double situation and its contradictions should be researched.

On the one hand we should look to societal changes to understand the meaning of and reality of young adults. Perhaps today's societal demands for a high level of individual competence is the motor of the development of young adults.

On the other hand we have to look for the consequences of these changes in youth life and young adult life. The demands on young adults and the way they create their own life-style are closely coherent. They develop lifestyles to master a new reflexivity on social possibilities and individual competence. We may speak about strategies for their new situation which hold them in a prolonged youth situation either as "students" or "young unemployed". *The strategies become the new lifestyle as it appears in sexual relations, work relations and especially in leisure-time contexts.*

At the same time, young adult strategies are not free of choice. Young adults are placed in tough competition with each other, competition in terms of job and future, which today is becoming more and more individualised. The collapse of the structure of political and class society and the development of individualistic competition may call for action. The development and problems of individual competence should perhaps be monitored more seriously in the future.

References

Alexander, C.J. 1987: *Twenty Lectures.* Columbia University Press. Cal.
Ariès, Ph. 1973: *Centuries of Childhood.* London
Clarke, J. et al. 1976: "Subcultures, Cultures and Class" in: Hall & Jeffersen: *Resistance through Rituals.* London
Cohen, P. 1972: "Subcultural conflict and Working Class Community". in *Working Papers in Culutral Studies.* nr 2. University of Birmingham.
Dreier, O. 1993: *Psykosocial behandling.* Dansk psykologisk forlag. Copenhagen.
Frønes, I & O. Stafseng. 1982. in Bjurstrøm, E: Generasjonsopprøret. Universitetsforlaget. Oslo.
Giddens, A. 1987: *The Constitution of Society.* Polity Press. Oxford
Giddens, A. 1991: *Modernity and Self-identity.* Polity. Oxford
Heritage, C.J. 1984: *Garfinkel and Ethnomethodology.* Polity Press. Oxford.
Heritage, C.J. 1987: Ethnomethodology. In: Giddens & Turner (eds) *Social Theory Today.* Stanford, Cal.
Hollingshead, A.B. 1949: *Elmtown's Youth.* N.Y.
Holzkamp, K 1983: *Grundlegung der Psychologie.* Campus. Frankfurt.
Mørch, S. 1985: *At forske i Ungdom.* Rubikon. Copenhagen
Mørch, S. 1993: *Projektbogen.* Rubikon. Copenhagen
Mørch, S. 1991:Youth reproduced and investigated. In: Ehrnrooth, J & L. Siural: *Construction of Youth.* VAPK. Helsingi.
Mørch, S. 1994: Une theorie de la Jeuness. In: Hudon, R & B. Fournier: *Jeunesses et politique.* L'Harmatten. Paris
Mørch, S. & S. Frost 1993: Pedagogical intervention and youth development. in Engelsted(ed): *The Sociatal Subject.* Århus. Denmark
Mørch, S. & S. Frost, H. Sieling, S. Lauersen 1994: *Ungdomsliv og ungdomsklubben.* BUPL. Copenhagen.
Mørch, S. 1995: Culture and the Challenge of Adaptation: Foreign Youth in Denmark. In: *International Journal of Comparative Race and Ethnic Studies.* De Sitter. Ontario. Canada.
Musgrove, F. 1965: *Youth and Social Order.* Indiana.
Nelleman, A.H. 1966): *Den Danske Skoles Historie.* (Reprint) København
Sève, L. 1978: *Marxisme og personlighedsteori.* Rhodos Copenhagen. (French edition: Édition Sociales. Paris 1974)
Tolman, C.W. & W. Maiers (eds) 1991: *Critical Psychology.* Cambridge University Press.

A Strategy for the Development of a Theory of Organisational Leadership and Administration

OLE ELSTRUP RASMUSSEN

The theoretical problem

During the course of recent decades there has been, within the field of organisation theory, an ongoing discussion as to what extent leadership and administration[1] are different organisational phenomena (e.g. Zaleznik, 1977). The distinction sought was, however, not given a proper definition until the appearance of the influential book *Leaders* by Bennis and Nanus (1985). Here leadership was defined as "path finding" and administration as "path following", a difference which is cleverly expressed by Bennis in the sentence: "Leaders are people who do the right thing; managers are people who do things right."

Yet even though it is becoming traditional to distinguish between leadership and administration, there is still anything but agreement on just what it means to lead and to administer. Questions such as: who is competent or qualified to lead and administer, and how should such leadership and administration be handled with regard to both efficacy and efficiency, remain unanswered.

Within the field of leadership research there exists a now classic tradition of seeking the abilities, i.e. qualifications, the true leader has, without regard to whether the individual concerned is seen as a leader or administrator.

The study of leadership abilities as a discipline was first subjected to a thorough, although not fatal, critique by Stokdill (1948). His criticisms were subsequently followed by others, especially from the area of entrepreneurship research, which can be regarded as a special branch of leadership study

---

[1] The terms leadership, management and adminstration are used interchangably in the literature. In the following discussion the term administration will be used for both management and administration. Where the theories make no distinction between administration, management and leadership, the term leadership will be used.

(Czarniawska-Joerges & Wolff, 1991). A. H. van de Ven (1980) thus points out that there is no empirical evidence to confirm the existence of a finite number of leader abilities, nor have any abilities been discovered which make it possible to differentiate between the successful leader and the unsuccessful. Gartner (1989) even goes so far as to maintain that the theory of personal abilities is based on posing the research question in the wrong way. Instead of asking who the entrepreneur/leader is, we should be asking what it is the entrepreneur/leader is doing.

The idea of understanding what leaders do, instead of who and what they are, can be traced back to a very extensive research undertaken by researchers at Ohio State University and Michigan University. On the basis of a number of questionnaires and using factor analysis, they arrived at the conclusion that in their activities, leaders are either relation- or task-oriented. Probably the best-known consequence of this work is the managerial grid of Blake and Mouton (1964), where relation and task orientations intersect as more-or-less dimensions in a system consisting of 3 x 3 categories. Blake's and Mouton's conception of leadership was a hit in managerial circles, but was heatedly criticised by academics, partly because there is no empirical evidence to support the model, and partly because the model pays no attention to the fact that leaders necessarily require others to lead.

At the same time, the style of leadership line of inquiry was given new life when researchers set out to investigate to what extent those being led could be incorporated into the model, especially with respect to personal influence on the decision-making process. Thus Muczyk and Reimann (1987), for example, developed a leadership model which included "the dimensions of involvement": autocratic-democratic and permissive-directive. The problem is, however, that those being led never enter the picture as influential persons, but are merely defined as more or less of an influence. The category system has also been criticised for not taking situational factors into account. Fiedler (1967), with his Contingency Theory, and Hersey and Blanchard (1988), with their Situational Leadership Theory, among others have attempted to rectify this shortcoming. But as the situational theories, like the others, ultimately rest upon the claim that leader behaviour derives from leader abilities, and that the behaviour of those being led derives from follower abilities, for example, in the form of maturity, the differences between ability-, activity- and situation-oriented leadership theories can hardly be described as major ones.

On the basis of an analysis of several analogous entrepreneurship theories I wrote (Elstrup Rasmussen, 1994a, p.14):

It might seem strange that activity theories are not so different from ability theories. Considered in an epistemological perspective, however, the reason for the fundamental similarities appears. Both paradigms build on the same logical foundation. The activity theories do not pose the question: what does the entrepreneur do, but: what is the activity of the entrepreneur? The activity theories follow exactly the same patterns as the ability theories when building systematics of human action. The only difference between the two paradigms is that the ability theories systematise the *causes* of individual action, while the activity theories systematise the *results* of individual action.

I am of the opinion that the same conclusion can be reached concerning the category-oriented leadership theories. At the same time I regard the ability, activity and situation theories as arbitrary constructs, which have not shown themselves to be well-suited to explain what it entails for a leader to find or an administrator to follow a path, because leadership and administration in these theories become, in the final analysis, abstract sets of categories and causal relations, posited through a common-sense interpretation.

There are, of course, other approaches to the study of leadership processes such as, for example, French and Raven (1959), whose classical power theory has most recently been further extended in the work of Yukl (1989). Here Yukl constructs, primarily on the basis of a series of paper and pencil investigations, two types of power: position power and personal power, each of which covers four subcategories. Besides the fact that Yukl's system of categories is not founded on any real theory of leadership, his and other similar systems also share the problem that the division between the "super-individual position" and "personal power" creates several irresolvable contradictions, as demonstrated in Elstrup Rasmussen (1994a). Either the individual disappears, as is the case in Yukl's theory, to become the forms of power mentioned or follower commitment, compliance or resistance, is reconstructed in the form of needs, as claimed by McClelland (1971, 1975) with his contention that the need for achievement creates the entrepreneur and the need for power creates the leader. So that, despite the fact that this type of theory attempts to describe irrefutable organisational processes, such as power, there is little to indicate that this categorical-constructivist approach can result in a proper theory, either of leadership or administration.

In recent years attention has been directed towards the developmental aspect of leadership. Burns (1978) thus introduces the concept "transforming" into leadership theory, but it is Bass (1985) in particular who, in distinguishing between transactional and transformational leadership, manages to point out the need to include a concept of development in leadership theory. But even though he succeeds in this, the result becomes categorical as developed on the basis of his Multifactor Leadership Questionnaire. Due to the factor-analytical foundation of the theory it never goes beyond its own typology of forms of transformation. The most interesting aspect of the theory development by Bass, to my mind, is his creation of a connection going all the way back to Weber's (1972) classical interpretation of charisma, and thus to the innovative entrepreneur, as he is described by the school of thought founded by Schumpeter (1931). In Bass (1985), theories of leadership and entrepreneurship have become a common field which, at a high level of generalisation, could be said to cover setting up an organisation by means of entrepreneurship, maintaining the operations of an organisation by means of administration, and transforming an organisation by means of leadership. But this has not lead to any clarification of the situation in the field of research. Researchers still approach the leader and administrator just as the entrepreneur who, as Kilby (1972) says, is like the heffalump in Winnie the Pooh, i.e. a large and rather important animal, whom many people claim to have seen. Whom some even claim to be able to describe roughly. For whom traps have been laid for a long time, but who unfortunately has never fallen into any of these traps, for which reason the searching proceeds unabated.

To my mind the problems of research in leadership and administration are caused by the fact that scholars have not until now been in a position to make a theoretical distinction between the discursive development of *qualifications*, which form the basis for administration, and the discursive development of *competence*, which is the basis of leadership. It is the aim of the following discussion to provide an outline of the way we can distinguish between qualifications and competence, and to demonstrate that this distinction makes it possible to develop a strategy for a discursive founding of organisational leadership and administration.

The paradigmatic problem

To understand how it is possible to distinguish between qualifications and competence, it is necessary to give a brief outline of the *means* used in the attempt to construct the previously mentioned theories.

The tools used by leadership theory to date have ideally been formal logic in the form in which the attempt has been made to apply it to classical, kinetic problems. Leadership theorists have attempted to take Newtonian mechanics as the paradigm for their research, or in other words they have assumed the existence of force fields which can causally determine the movements of points of mass in time and space. Scholars have thus assumed organisations and human thought to be kinetic systems which can be described through rule-based models in the same manner as science has succeeded in describing, for example, the earth's revolution around the sun. The best-known and purest example of leadership theorists for whom natural science represents the ideal are Taylor (1916) and Fayol (1946), who developed the first formal models of decision-making for the establishment of an organisation and the administrative maintenance of an organisation respectively, which on the whole set the basic tone for all later organisational thought. Within the discursive field of thought and language Piaget (1972) and Chomsky (1966), for instance, take considerably similar positions.

It is true, of course, that the various theorists mentioned above have emphasised different aspects of the organisation, such as human relations or individual characteristics, just as cognitive and linguistic scientists have had their controversies, but when it comes down to basics the assumption is that, even though organisations are perhaps not completely identical with mass-based systems, they are still rational systems which can be modelled with the help of formal logic. And should it not prove possible to create models, this is due to the fact that the systems are too complicated for us to be able to compute at this point in time. Our theoretical problems are due to the fact that systems are *complicated*, not to the fact that the systems are incomputable because they are *complex*. The systems are thus in principle computable, and as human beings we can form a plan because we are rationally thinking beings by nature. But are we – always?

An example from Nisbett (1993) manages, in my opinion, to question the idea that we are naturally, i.e. basically, rationally thinking beings. It begins with the following experiment:

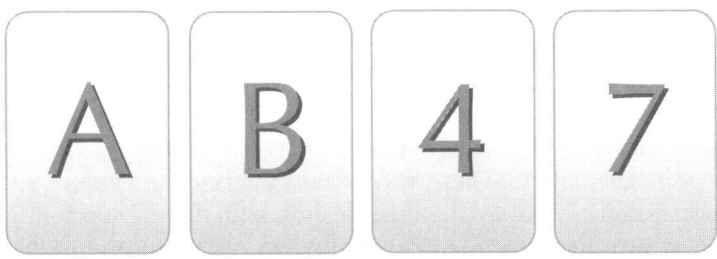

Fig. 1

Four cards are placed in front of the subject of the experiment, upon which are written A, B, 4 and 7. The subject is told that there is always a number on the opposite side of each letter and a letter on the opposite side of each number. The subject is then asked how many cards must be turned over to determine whether the following rule is broken:

If a card has an A on one side, it has a number 4 on the other.

If the reader, after thinking this over, answers two cards, i.e. A and 7, then he or she has correctly solved the problem. If the reader solves the problem, he or she belongs to the approximately 10 per cent of the population – all well-educated – who can, within a reasonable amount of time, solve the problem. If the problem is solved it is presumably because the problem-solver has spent a goodly portion of his or her existence studying formal logic, or because he or she knew the solution already.

But how is it that we cannot solve the simplest logical problems when our language, according to Chomsky, reflects a competence which is of a formally logical type, or which can at least be functionally described with the help of formal logic? And how can it be that it is so difficult to solve the problem, when the highest level of our human thought, according to Piaget, is also of a formally logical type? The answer can only be, as far as I can see, that the basic human thought processes are not of a formally logical type. We can think according to patterns of formal logic, but this we only do when we orient ourselves in a specific manner. This does not necessarily mean, however, that our organisations cannot be perfectly rational. Allow me, however, to offer an example of an organisation which indicates the opposite:

The directors of a large, Danish publicly owned enterprise, hired a consulting firm to rationalise one of its departments. This department was inefficient, in the opinion of the directors, because there was not 100 per cent certainty as to who should do what and when. Extremely precise job descriptions were drawn up, along with logical flow charts; analyses were made of the way in which data, workers and administrators should interact in a rational and friction-free manner. In the thoroughly rationalised department, however, the entire system collapsed the first time it ran into an unexpected situation. There was, naturally, no one to deal with the unexpected when it occurred, because dealing with the unexpected was not included in any job function. Rationality, in short, took a tumble the moment what has been called in organisational theory the "glue" of the organisation, or its informal organisation, was removed. This informal organisation is something that no one can really define, but that everyone knows from practical experience is what holds the organisation together behind the rationality. And it is this something behind the rationality – what could be called sense – which forms the basis of competence.

It is gradually dawning on the rationalists that there is something else, which is a premise for rationality but which they cannot describe with the help of the tools previously employed. Thus Putnam (1989) demonstrates with exquisite clarity that his own previously functionalist concept of re-presentation and reality on a logical basis is not tenable, and that now we must search for something that he can not properly define, while Johnson (1992) shows that a deeper meaning must exist than can be expressed in analytical terms. Johnson feels that these depths can be found in the natural embeddedness of the body in the world. But as far as I can see, both Putnam's and Johnson's revolts remain within the framework of rationalism. They do not manage to point out that a deeper sense could exist, the sense of innovation, which cannot be described with the help of an algorithm but through what could be termed a logic of action.

I do not deny that human beings can be rational and perform actions and construct systems which follow a formally logical thinking pattern, and which can, therefore, be modelled within formal logic. I maintain, however, that it is not this process which comprises the foundation of human thinking and human organising.

The ability to use formal logic is a *qualification* which humans can develop, while the ability to make sense through innovation, which we must be able to model in terms of one form or another of logic of action, is the true *competence* of human beings.

Distinguishing qualification from competence

But what, to be more precise, is the difference between qualifications and competence, and how can human competence be studied?

I do not intend to go into detail here on how the theory of discontinuity (Elstrup Rasmussen, 1994b) establishes the theoretical basis for distinguishing between qualifications and competence. I only wish to mention that the theory includes both a general and a specific part. In the general discontinuity theory the implicate[2] order of human existence is modelled within the limits defined by the following degrees of freedom: difference, time-space, development and self-reference. The theory thus presumes that differences do exist, that differences in the form of human ideas and objects exist and develop because of human self-reference, in time and space. Within human discourse, for example, ideas can be identified with other ideas and form more general ideas, just as ideas can be synthesised with other ideas to form new ideas.

The specific discontinuity theory includes three fundamental processes of development: the process by which individuals place their own lives in perspective, the process by which individuals order their lives, and the process by which individuals organise their own lives in relation to and as part of the interactions which comprise human existence. It is with the help of these fundamental developmental processes that the individual is able to create sense in his existence, that sense which is the prerequisite for the establishment of systemativity in that same existence.

In the following section I shall define qualifications and competence and describe the most important characteristics of these two theoretical constructs.

Definition: A qualified personal performance is an unfolding of knowledge, insight and values, which systematises a complicated occurrence, in such a way that a specific state of objective is achieved.

When we speak of qualifications, we are dealing with the way in which we as human beings systematically unfold knowledge, insight and values. Human beings are capable of categorising their world ideally as well as materially, and to combine these categories to form systematics. This we can do in either the form of machines or algorithms and administrative systems. The ability to systematise is, in fact, one of the reasons for the great success of the human race. By systematising itself in its own network human beings are able to maintain a *high rate of repetition*. We can reproduce ourselves with a very high degree of certainty. This manner of action has become the focus of greatest attention in western industrialised culture, where repetition and standardisation has served as an important source of economic prosperity.

---

[2] The term "implicate order" is borrowed from Bohm (1990) but does not have the same theoretical meaning. Implicate order is described in the theory of discontinuity with the aid of Thom's (1975) theory of catastrophes.

In order to be competitive, industry must, however, always keep abreast of developments, as it is called. And this can only be achieved if individuals, and consequently enterprises, remain flexible, i.e. forgo regularity, abandon repetition and place their emphasis on innovation instead on the ability to change, in other words on conditions which are made possible by human competence.

But what is it then, that individual human beings can accomplish, singly or in groups, which is not merely systematisation and repetition? My answer is: humans can create sense in a complex situation, and the function which ensures that this is made possible is what I call competence.

Definition: A competent personal performance is an assembly of ideas that perspectivises, orders and organises a complex occurrence in such a way that a sense making state is brought about.

In order to arrive at just how this sense making state is brought about, it is necessary to provide a brief description of some technical presuppositions from the theory of discontinuity.

The point of departure is that human existence forms a complex network, within which ideas and objects are constantly being developed. In this network the development of ideas and objects, i.e. networking, appears as a complex flow which the individual person or group must handle. The handling of a complex flow of ideas and objects I call a discourse. A discourse is comprised of a series of occurrences, where an occurrence is thus identical with the handling of a finite, complex flow of ideas and objects. The space of the discourse is that of human existence which, as previously mentioned, is the space which is determined by the degrees of freedom, difference, time-space, development and self-reference.

Human beings basically deal with and create, co-operatively and as individual persons, the flow of ideas and the flow of objects in the same manner; the only difference is that ideas are created and dealt with through the medium of language, which can appear in the form of sentences and texts. In the following discussion I shall only be concerned with the sentential and textual handling of ideas.

With considerable simplification we can say that the individual person treats the flow of ideas, in which he or she takes part, by means of the three mechanisms of the competence function: ordering, organising and perspectivising. These three mechanisms in combination comprise the sentence-creating assembling mechanism of competence. In other words, the three mechanisms co-operatively create natural language by assembling

(Aa(AaO)) strings, which are quite common sentences of the form: (he (*A*gent) sees (*a*ction) that (she (*A*gent) eats (*a*ction) a bun (*O*bjective))). In our everyday lives we are unaware of possessing this sentence-assembling competence function. What we are aware of, when the competence function is "running" is ourselves as the "I". "I" am my competence, where the primary function of competence is the ability to create sense by assembling sentences. We can also say that the person, as I, reconstructs the complex flow of ideas into sentences which make sense.

The point of departure for the assembling of natural language, i.e. sentences, is the idea. Ideas make their appearance as words when we speak or write. For example, the idea "horse" exists in our minds and in our networking, that is, in our culture. This "horse-idea" is given expression when we hear or speak the word horse. Ideas are being constantly reproduced and further developed in the *ordering process*. Just how this, according to the theory of discontinuity, actually takes place, is not so important here; what is of interest for us is merely that the ordering of ideas appears in natural language as words. The reader can, meanwhile, attempt to conceive of ordering as a process in which everything connected, for example, with the word horse is transformed into a prototype, i.e. that of the "horse-idea".

The ideas which are created in the ordering process are *organised* while we speak, so that some ideas appear as *Agents* (A) while others appear as *actions* (a) and yet others as *Objectives* (O). For example, "The horse (A) drinks (a) water (O)".

The final function, *perspectivising*, sees to it that the objective, which includes everything following the verb, is divided up through the use of prepositions in such a manner that a sentence of natural language will have a figure, a ground, a means and a goal. To give an example: The farmer (A) splits (a) the firewood (O_{figure}) on the block (O_{ground}) with an axe (O_{means}) for the winter (O_{goal}).

>   (A) The farmer
>   (a) splits
>   (O_f) the firewood
>   (O_g) on the block
>   (O_m) with an axe
>   (O_{go}) for the winter

Such a sentence is clearly action-oriented. The sentence expresses the making sense of life, or a meaning in life, if you will. We could also say that the sentence is a formatting of the flow of ideas into discourse, or that when we speak, we intentionally set a number of constraints which combine ideas into meaning. It is thus not the case that we first think in order to subsequently speak. We think while speaking and speak while thinking, not to pronounce sentences concerning a reality which is something apart from ourselves, but in order to exist discursively in our human condition. In a certain sense we think the world in the same manner as Gibson (1979) maintains we perceive it, i.e. in motion. The sentences of natural language are meaningful (sense-making) in the discourse in which they are expressed and not, as analytical linguistics maintains (e.g. Tarski, 1944), something which appears as meaning in relation to an object. Human beings can, of course, if they put themselves into a specific systematising mode, deal with the world according to the rules of formal logic, but this mode is, as Putnam (1989) points out, not fundamental.

But what is most important here is that the sentence is an organising and putting into perspective of a series of ordered ideas, which as intentional constraints make sense of an occurrence. With the assistance of natural language we manage to assemble the stream of ideas – and objects as well – into a structure which includes something we are acting upon: the figure, something the figure is anchored in: the ground, something we wish to achieve and see in the future: the goal, and, finally, something we wish to make use of to move toward the goal: the means.

All the sentences in our natural language are in principle built up in this way. And it is this which is the fundamental human competence. The individual human being can in a sense making manner manage to create meaning, i.e. create a focused in-perspective coherence in an occurrence through the set of ideas he or she makes use of in the occurrence. And, in making sense, the ideas which serve as the basis for the continuing formation of meaning are developed further through competence. The individual person develops him- or herself through sense making or innovatively, if you will, by constantly creating meaning in discourse, and the more ideas the individual makes use of, which are relevant for the given occurrence, the more competently the person acts.

When the complexity of the flow of ideas and accordingly of the occurrence is not too great, meaning can be created through the assembling of individual and isolated natural sentences. When the complexity of the flow increases, in accordance with the occurrence becoming more complex, it ceases to be possible to create meaning through individual sentences. In harmony with their increasing the complexity of the flow of ideas, human beings have developed an extra degree of freedom in dealing with this flow, i.e. the ability to assemble texts which, in contrast to individual sentences, are characterised by the setting of intentional constraints in the form of half and full stops and parenthetical phrases, for example.

I shall later return to how it is possible, with the help of perspective text analysis[3], to describe meaning on the basis of an entire text.

The action-logical way of thinking which lies behind the understanding of the transition from manipulating the idea flow through individual sentences to dealing with it through text production can perhaps best be illustrated with the help of an analogy. If we observe a falling leaf[4], we notice that when it begins to fall the leaf vibrates. This vibration is a manifestation of the energy being dissipated through the leaf. We could say that in vibrating, the leaf is disposing of the energy created by the interaction of the two force fields generated by the forces of gravity and of air resistance respectively. In a similar fashion the speaking person disposes of the complexity of the idea flow by creating constraints through the assembling of sense making sentences. By verbally formulating something which is complex, the degree of complexity is reduced.

If the leaf continues to fall the energy it must dispose of increases. At a certain level vibrating is no longer sufficient; as a result the leaf begins to sway from side to side like a pendulum. In a similar fashion the person must begin to create texts when the complexity, which the individual concerned has contributed to in creating sentences, becomes too great to be dealt with through individual sentences. The person has, like the leaf, activated an extra degree of freedom, which in humans is a developmental product which they themselves have made necessary. Unlike the leaf, people, because of the self-referential nature of human existence, is themselves involved in creating the complexity which they then must dispose of through texts. Within the sphere of human existence, human beings create problems for themselves which they themselves solve.

When it is no longer possible for the leaf to swing back and forth to escape from its dissipation problems, it begins to rotate, after which the leaf has no more degrees of freedom to activate. I believe that the degree of freedom which the human being activates, once the text no longer suffices to "dissipate" the complexity, is organisation, which primarily involves leadership, a strategy for the understanding of which I intend to attempt to develop.

---

[3] Perspective text analysis was developed at Lund University by Bernhard Bierschenk and Inger Bierschenk and transformed into a PC-based solution model by Helge Helmersson.

[4] A complete physical description of the falling leaf is given in Kugler and Turvey (1987).

We can thus conceive of sentences, texts and leadership as forms of stabilising constraints, and of competence as the mechanism which creates these forms of stability in a discourse of increasing complexity.

As can be seen, the *qualification function* differs radically from the *competence function*. With the help of qualifications humans can systematise complicated occurrences in such a manner that they can be said to solve problems. With the help of competence on the other hand, humans can create meaning in complex occurrences in such a manner that they can be said to introduce perspectives in the form of figure, ground, objective and means into the occurrences. Allow me to give a simple example. When I head into town to buy groceries for my evening meal, I am solving a very simple problem, for which I am qualified because I have the knowledge and insight necessary to go shopping. When I as a Dane pay what is written on the price tag, I make use of a knowledge and insight which systematises myself in relation to the goods and the proprietor of the shop. It is my qualification that I am capable of repeating something which for Danes is such a well-known systematic, that of commerce as an exchange of money for goods, this in turn implies that I know that I shall receive a specific product if I pay a specific sum of money. But since I am, for example, qualified in a special Danish fashion, it is very difficult for me to carry out systematised transactions if I find myself in a different culture where I am forced to haggle over the price. Since I have no systematic which makes it possible for me to carry out the transaction in a qualified fashion I deal with the situation through competence. Instead of making use of known systematic forms, I organise and order my ideas into a specific perspective so that the complicated situation becomes meaningful to me. If I am successful in creating meaning and this results in a purchase, I have at the same time created the premises for a systematic, so that I can at another time act in a similar situation by repetition. The sense created is maintained as a systematic.

If there is no opportunity of making sense in the unknown situation, all development is arrested. This is, in my opinion, what went wrong with the reorganization of the department of the public enterprise discussed previously. In striving to create a rational organisation those who intervened failed to see that, by systematising everything down to the smallest detail, they made the unfolding of competence difficult. They denied the human beings the space to make sense of occurrences which were not systematised, or which cannot be systematised because they have not or cannot assume the character of repetition.

Making sense and text analysis

Making sense by means of competence at the level of the text can be modelled with the help of perspective text analysis (inter alia Bierschenk, I. (1992), Bierschenk, B. (1993), Elstrup Rasmussen (1994c)). In the following section I will not go into the technical aspects of perspective text analysis, but merely give a simple example of how this method makes it possible to distinguish between the meaning which the person sets as the figure and that which is set as the ground. I shall at the same time illustrate how the perspectivist text-based introduction to the study of the person is distinct from the analytical test-based, in order to show in what way the action-logical introduction to the study of human sense is distinct from the analytically-logical introduction to human rationality, which as previously mentioned is the main angle of approach in the leadership theories discussed, and in general have all one form or another of analytical paper and pencil tests as their empirical foundation.

The case I intend to focus upon involves promotion. A large Danish enterprise hired a consulting firm to evaluate whether one of their highly creative employees was suited to be promoted to the position of leader of his department. The evaluation involved a personality test, interviews by a psychologist, the employee's self-evaluation of his own strong and weak points, and a text written by the candidate. This text included a description of how the candidate regarded the job for which he was being considered. Under the heading of "leadership" the candidate described how he conceived of leadership. It is this "leadership section" I have subjected to a perspective text analysis.

I have chosen the example because I think it can be interesting to see how parts of a relatively comprehensive analytical test-based assessment turn out in comparison to a perspective text analysis. Needless to say, I did not have access to the assessment of the consulting firm until after the analysis had been completed.

The traditional assessment

A personality test was used in connection with the assessment of the candidate. The test results are shown in Figure 2. They show, for example, that the candidate has made 10 positive choices on the dimension independence. These positive choices are a low score for this dimension, whose normal range stretches from 10 to 15, as indicated by the bar in the model. As the model reveals, the candidate records extreme scores for all dimensions, with the exception of adaptability.

On the basis of the test, a personal interview with the candidate, an intelligence test and the candidate's description of his purpose of leadership, the psychologist drew up the following key-word theory of the mental make-up of the candidate:

He is very perceptive, and he is creative. Signals come to him from every corner of his surroundings. He picks up and processes the signals in a more or less uncensored manner.

He has a comprehensive outlook, and he is good at supporting, inspiring and motivating people. He will be an inspiring 'here and now' leader, but, because of personal insecurity and personal weaknesses that express themselves in many different and unstable ways, he will encounter problems in more long-term tasks. As he has no great impact on people, he is only able to implement his creative ideas through others who have the drive to see his ideas through, or to do so himself through short bursts of incredibly hard work. He will throw himself into a task and forget every thing else, and then fall back into passivity for a period. In his style of leadership, he will be dependent on others. He will seek consensus, but he will also produce a court of favourites.

He is authoritarian and anti-authoritarian at the same time. In many cases, he will be able to compensate and act rationally because of his intelligence, but this will be in spite of his own insecurity.

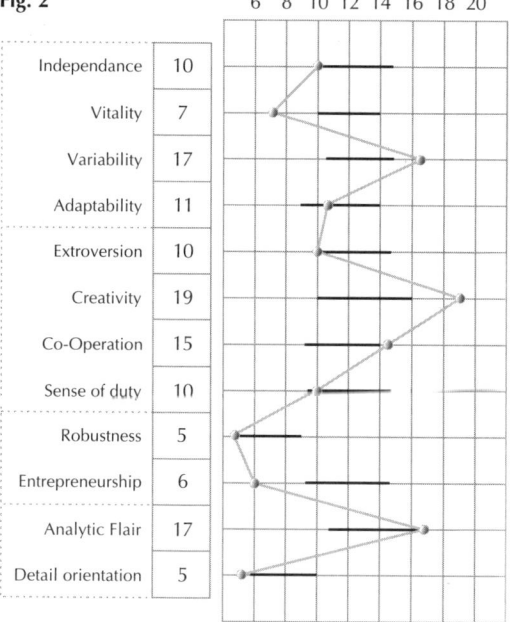

Fig. 2

The perspective text analysis assessment

The perspective analysis of the candidate which is made on the basis of a text of approx. 1.5 standard pages in length, includes a figure holophor (Figure 3, which is to be read counter-clockwise) and a ground holophor (Figure 5). Viewed as a whole, holophors of figure, ground, goal and means reveal the action-logical modelling of the meaning which is hidden in a given text.

The term "holophor" is a neologism created by integrating the terms "hologram" and "metaphor". Holophor means the bearer (phor) of an entirety (holo). The basis for the origin of the holophor is, as previously mentioned, a text, which is an assembling of sentences, which are assembled ideas. When the complexity of the idea flow becomes so great that the assembling of individual natural sentences is no longer sufficient to make sense of an occurrence, competence assembles texts. A text can be characterised as a system of sentences assembled with pauses and rests. Rests are created in the text, for example, through the use of half stops and pauses through the use of full stops.

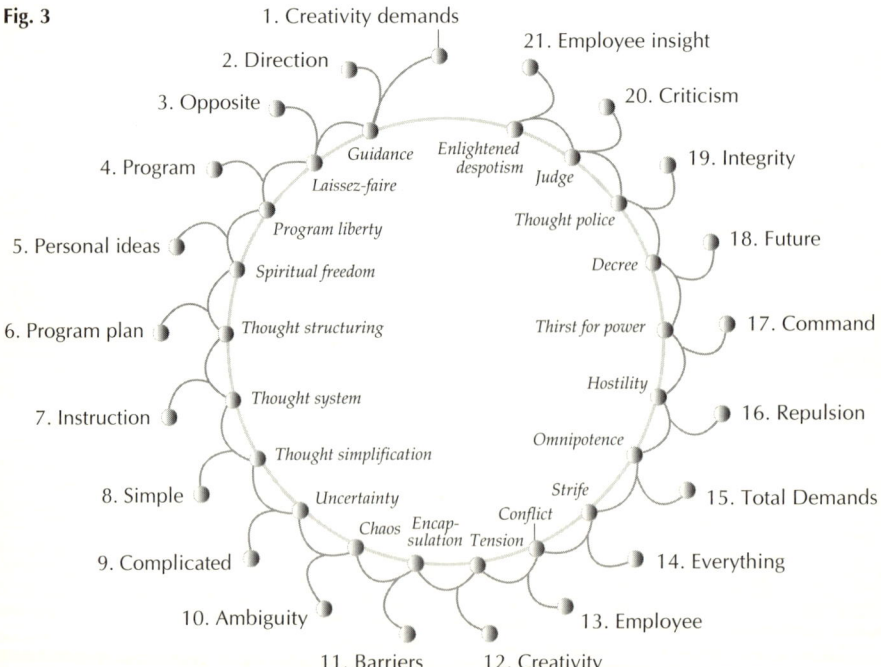

Fig. 3

What is interesting about the text assembling is its ability to create information on two levels: the morphological level and the level of ideas, and that these two levels interact, thus giving rise to the meaning of the holophor.

On the one information level: the morphological aspects appear in the holophor as a progressive, connected chain of stabilising states. We can think of the chain as a series of kinematic source-sink states (Kugler & Turvey, 1987), in which the resulting stable state itself becomes a sink in relation to a source.

Fig. 4

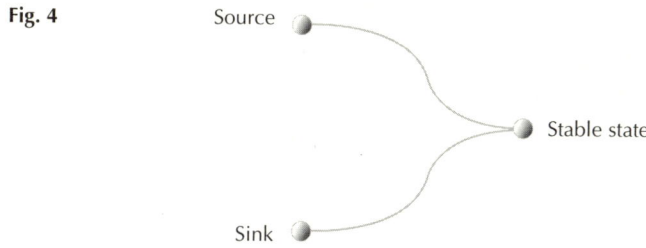

Figure 4 shows a single link in the morphology of the holophor. The relationship between "source" and "sink" expresses a potential difference, which stabilises itself as a "stable state", which is a kinematically equilibrium state in a flow. The model thus illustrates a system's movement toward stability. Such a system could, for example, consist of two gas containers which are connected to each other. If one of them originally contains many gas particles and the other few, the one with the many gas particles will be a source in relation to the other which will be a sink. Because there exists a potential difference between the two containers, a flow of gas particles from source to sink will be created. The flow will equalise the potential difference in such a way that the entire system will reach a stable state, in which the amount of gas particles in the two connected containers will be roughly the same.

Bierschenk and Bierschenk have, through a series of theoretical and experimental studies, shown that text assembling can be described at the grapheme level as a kinematic flow, which involves a series of stable states. What Bierschenk and Bierschenk have discovered is that the text, as a set of graphemes (letters and spaces between words), is assembled in such a fashion as to make it possible to describe the text as a kinematic system, which unfolds through a series of source-sink relationships which are given expression in a series of stable states. On this information level there is thus only a question of the text as a quantitative system of potentials, which can be described morphologically as a connected chain of source-sink relationships and stable states. In the chain as a whole the final stable state expresses the stability of the entire system. In Figure 3 the morphological final state of the holophor is designated as "Enlightened despotism".

We can also say that at this information level the holophor orders the flow of ideas, and the ordering is given expression in the model's morphology. In the example above the morphology of the holophor is very regular. In other holophors, up to three morphological levels have been observed.

It is important to keep in mind that the morphology of the holophor is determined wholly by the text assembling. The holophor's morphology contains no possibilities at all for interpretation.

The discovery by Bierschenk and Bierschenk that text production involves a quantifiable, informative morphology is unique within cognitive linguistics.

The morphology of the holophor, as understood by Bohm and Hiley (1993), is active information, which provides information to the second level of the holophor: the idea level. The means by which this occurs is twofold.

The first means of informing involves ordering. In the holophor of figure (Figure 3), which is to be read counter-clockwise, a numbered series of initial ideas can be seen. These initial ideas are, regarded morphologically, source states. Each of these states involves a set of graphemes, which appear as strings of words and phrases. The words and phrases involved in each source state, which as we have seen are determined by the text being analysed, are expressed as an entirety in the model through a named, prototypical idea. An example of such naming of a prototypical idea is "10. Ambiguity".

The other means of informing involves organising. Organising contains a series of inner syntheses (in italics) which, as morphologically stable states or sink states, bind the initial ideas together into a whole. The stable states of the holophor appear on the idea level as a series of virtual states which organise the flow of ideas. This part of the holophor's information includes, along with the syntheses, an element of argumentation. For example, the model in Figure 3 is to be read in such a way that the candidate's holophor of figure starts from "1. Creativity demands" and "2. Direction" which could be ordered by synthesis to fall under "control", where the argument for the synthesis is that demands and direction can both be encompassed by the idea "control". Since the synthetic argumentation itself is action-logical, the synthesis involves an element of "foreign" formation of meaning around the meaning-forming elements of the holophor. Meanwhile the degrees of freedom in the argumentation are limited to the choice of synonyms, since the initial ideas (the numbered source states) are directly text-dependent because of the words and word combinations which form the basis of the initial ideas. It is thus possible that the word "control" could be replaced with "administration", but it would not then be possible to use words such as "chaos" and "uncertainty" which occur elsewhere in the holophor.

One of the ways by which the degrees of freedom in argumentation can be reduced is by introducing constraints in the form of theories concerning the subject matter to which the holophor gives meaning. When working with "leadership" holophors it is thus important that the synthetic arguments should be integrated into the leadership theory which develops in the course of research on leadership through the perspective method.

As previously mentioned, we work our way around the holophor counter-clockwise. By constantly ordering ideas synthetically in a progressive process we ultimately reach the superordinate conception, which is described in the model as "enlightened despotism", which is the candidate's most pervasive idea of leadership, and which orders and organises all his other ideas.

The figure holophor does not, however, represent the candidate's entire conception of leadership. It also has a holophor of ground which is shown in Figure 5.

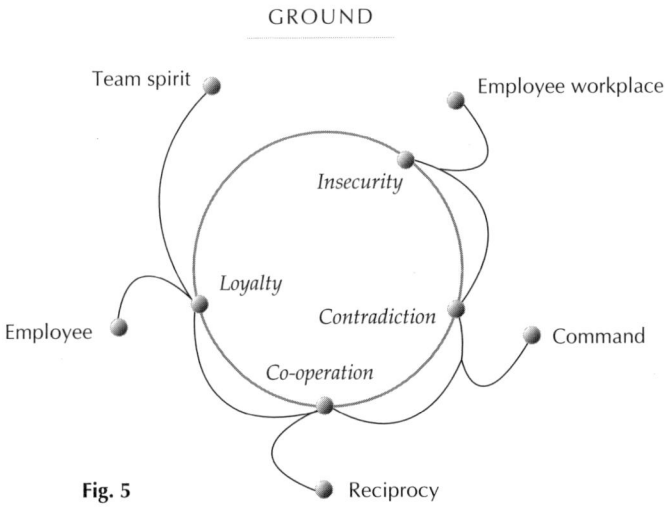

Fig. 5

The ground holophor is constructed according to the same principles as the figure holophor. It has, however, a more limited scope, which is the rule rather than the exception. It corresponds, for instance, to the case where in describing a room it is only necessary to mention a floor, upon which various pieces of furniture are placed. The predominant characteristic of the ground, upon which the candidate's figure stands, is "insecurity".

Comparisons
Since this action-logical leadership analysis is not integrated in an experimental design, which is controlled by a theory, it is only possible to comment on characteristics of the internal qualities of the model.

The ground holophor moves from "team spirit" to "loyality" through "co-operation" and "contradiction" to an all-embracing "insecurity", because the candidate concurrently conceives of leadership as "reciprocity" and "command".

It is quite interesting that the term "insecurity" is also used in the analytical, test-based description by the psychologist. There is, however, a difference between the analytically-logical and the action-logical contentions concerning the candidate. The analytically-logical introduction maintains that the candidate *is* insecure, which implies that he *has* a specific attribute which in itself indicates that he *will* be insecure as a leader. The action-logical introduction maintains that the most basic conception of the candidate concerning leadership can be called "insecurity", but not just any insecurity. The idea "insecurity" orders and organises "team spirit", "loyalty" etc. because of which the candidate can be regarded as feeling himself insecure. But he does not simply feel insecure, he does it for a specific reason. And the reason is apparently that he bases his ideas of leadership on the contradiction between "reciprocity" and "command" without any mediating ideas. "Insecurity" is thus concrete and based in the synthetic model.

A form af insecurity also makes an appearance in the figure holophor where terms of freedom and control alternate constantly, because of which one might consider that the candidate, since he cannot manage to convincingly piece together his ideas of control and freedom, solves the conflict by means of "enlightened despotism".

The analytical introduction also noted a type of despotic position in the candidate, as the psychological analysis maintained that the candidate would keep a retinue. The analytical introduction also suggests that the court has a specific objective, i.e. the implementation of the candidate's creative ideas. The action-logical model shows, on the contrary, that even if creativity is felt to be an initial requirement, creativity disappears in the conflict between control and freedom.

In many respects it appears as if the action-logical and analytically-logical models catch, to a certain extent, the same mental aspects of the person, but as the last example shows, quite a decisive difference exists. In the analytical model each feature carries the same weight and occupies the same location in the model, which for example could mean that "creativity" remains a potent attribute throughout the entire analytical model, while "creativity" in the action-logical model is modified until the idea is practically nullified in "enlightened despotism".

This difference is vital, at least for anyone wishing to employ the person concerned. The employer was interested in promoting this highly creative employee to a leadership position with the aim of increasing the creativity of the entire department. On the basis of the analytical testing an employer could continue to believe that, even if the candidate would not become the most outstanding of leaders, he would in any case continue to express his own creative talent, eventually through others. And would perhaps be willing to take a chance on him. On the basis of the perspective analysis the conclusion would be drawn that all creativity would be smothered by uncertainty and dominance. And the employer would scarcely be likely to take that chance.

Perspective text analysis thus has several scientific qualities which the analytical tests do not have, because the method can discover connections which in analytical testing can only be brought out by common sense interpretations. To my mind, perspective text analysis, as part of a longitudinal research process, would be an exceptionally effective method of discovering mental changes, for example in connection with leadership development programmes.

Leadership and administration

Taking this as the starting point, it is then possible to create a strategy for the development of a theory of leadership and administration. But before outlining a model of organising, allow me a few words on what I feel comprises an enterprise or institution.

As illustrated in Figure 6, I conceive of an enterprise as something which is created in and is the creator of a complex flow of ideas and objects. By sucking in ideas and objects at one end and pumping out ideas and objects at the other, the enterprise creates and maintains itself in the flow. The flow of ideas and objects is the enterprise's energy, so to speak, while the complexity of the flow, as previously mentioned, is a necessity of the organising process.

Organising can be illustrated by observing streams of energy in systems which are either far from or close to equilibrium (Prigogine & Stengers, 1993). When the energy streams at far from equilibrium, it produces complex forms of organisation in the same way that a stream of water flowing swiftly produces whirlpools. When energy streams at close to equilibrium, it produces a steady movement.

At close to equilibrium, which in terms of human existence corresponds to low complexity, it is possible to deal with the flow of ideas and objects with the help of qualifications that, as will subsequently be shown, are a part of administration. This steady, low-complexity flow can be systematised, even dealt with practically on an assembly line, as the flow is sucked into the enterprise and pumped out again in transformed form, illustrated in the model in Figure 6 as movement through a pentagon. When the stream, on the other hand, is far from equilibrium, which means that the flow of ideas and objects exceeds the degree of complexity which can be dealt with by personal competence, the competence which is coupled to leadership steps in, as illustrated in the model in Figure 6 as a movement through a ring. It is only with the aid of competence that the human being is capable of transforming the bubbling stream of ideas and objects into coherent meaning. Through competence, human beings can renew themselves and their environment and in so doing transform the basis for their very survival, but when the complexity becomes very great personal competencies must be organised.

Fig. 6

It is, as previously said, my conception that the organisation just as the natural sentence and the natural text is a response to growing complexity in the flow of ideas. Human discourse quite simply becomes more and more complex, as a result of which humans must develop tools to be comfortable within it. I thus maintain that it must be possible to understand organisations as a degree of freedom developed in human existence to deal with the increased complexity of the flow of ideas and objects produced in human existence. It is the increase in the evolution of human existence itself which makes organisation an order of the day.

But since all human beings, according to present theory, are both qualified and competent, in one manner or another, how can we distinguish, for example, between the competence of the individuals in control and those being controlled?

The initial response to this question must be negative. There cannot be any difference in principle between, for example, the competence of a leader and the competence of participants, as modern human beings are competent in their own lives. The distinction between "leader" and "participant" must lie in another direction. Or there must be a limiting condition for competence, which can define one sort as leader competence and another sort as participant competence.

In the present theory one must obviously search for two limiting conditions: one which can create a difference between qualifications and another which can create a difference between competencies.

I think that "gradient of eigenvalue" is the limiting condition, which enables us to distinguish between leader competence and participant competence, while "gradient of dominance" is the limiting condition which makes it possible to distinguish between administrative qualifications and work qualifications.

The concept of eigenvalue refers to the worth of the adult person, detached from attachment. Attachment is an empirically grounded concept (Bowlby, 1969; Ainsworth & Bowlby, 1991), which refers to the trust shown by individuals in certain instances towards certain other individuals. The detachment of this attachment, that is, eigenvalue refers to the self-referential worth of the singular person developed through attachment. The eigenvalue gradient, thus, referes to differences in the field of eigenvalues in an occurrence.

Dominance refers to the obedience shown by individuals in certain instances and suggestions of certain other individuals. Using these definitions it is then possible to outline a preliminary model of organisation. This model includes both leadership and administration.

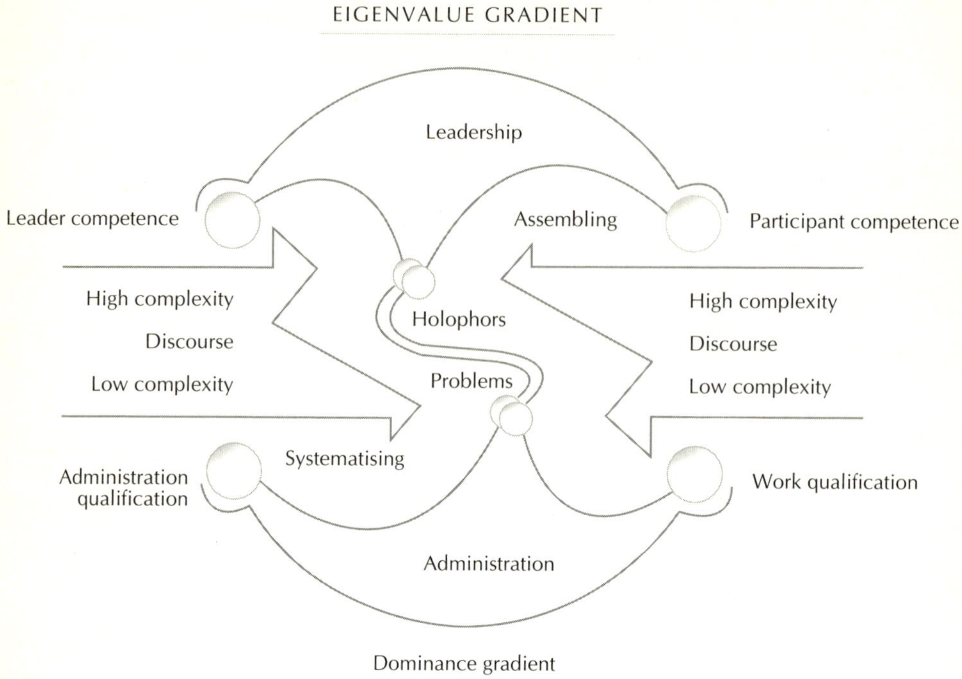

EIGENVALUE GRADIENT

Fig. 7

The model in Figure 7 is to be read in the following manner: where the flow of ideas and objects, i.e. the discourse, is highly complex, the individual person by his competence assembles his existence as a holophor. In the organising context, however, the position of the individual in the field af eigenvalues is determined by the existence of differences in eigenvalues. The individuals associated with relatively lower eigenvalues appear as participants, while individuals associated with relatively higher eigenvalues appear as leaders[5].

The "downward gradient" will never fail to appear in the participant's holophor, just as the opposite gradient will appear in the leader's holophor.

The result is a participant's and a leader's holophor which, due to the limiting condition of the eigenvalue gradient, will be fundamentally different.

To set this fundamental difference, i.e. to categorise, is not the same, however, as to have developed a theory of the means by which this

---

[5] I believe that it is the eigenvalue gradient that Weber (1972) described as charisma.

difference can deal with a flow of ideas more complex than the assembling of textual holophors. We need a strategy for the development of such a theory.

The strategy which I find to be most promising was developed by Kugler and Turvey (1987) in their attempt to create a theory to explain how motion patterns are intentionally co-ordinated. In the present context, the strategy will be to regard holophors as patterns, which co-operate at the micro level under the limiting condition of an eigenvalue gradient. Co-operation at the micro level creates co-ordination at the macro level, appearing in the form of a virtual holophor which, in Bohm's understanding, (1993) supplies information to the personal holophors. The virtual holophor is shown in the model in Figure 7 as "leadership". The strategic conception is thus to understand leadership as a continuous process, in which personal holophors determine and are informed by the ordering and organising morphology of the virtual holophor under the given limiting condition of the eigenvalue gradient.

Where the flow of ideas and objects is of low complexity, for example because competence has simplified something complicated by placing constraints in the form of sentences, text and leadership, the individual person through his qualifications systematises his existence into problems, i.e. the individual in a systematic fashions sets himself or herself problems and solves them. In the organisational context, however, the problem-solving of individuals is determined by the dominance gradient. The persons who have been positioned as dominant appear as administrators and their qualifications accordingly as administrative qualifications. Because the dominance gradient exists the dominant person's, i.e. the administrator's, systematisation in the form of his or her problems serves as the context within which his or her co-workers systematise their problems. As a result the administrator's problems, due to the dominance gradient, serve as a limiting condition for the worker's problem. This is not a question of the administrator's problems becoming those of the participants, but only that the administrator's problems set the context for those of his or her co-workers.

This sphere, which encompasses the dominance relationship between worker and administrator, the administrator's systematisation of problems and the workers systematisation of problems within the limiting condition imposed by the administrator, I refer to as administration. Administration is the form within which the organisation created through leadership is maintained as an organisation.

Conclusion

In conclusion it is important that I point out that through the theory of discontinuity and perspective text analysis, it has been shown clearly that the main body of all psychology and organisation theory is concerned with a limited portion of human existence. Classical psychology and organisation theory is concerned principally with systematised human existence, in which and for which the individual can qualify him- or herself. But in recent years more and more researchers are realising that they have failed to grasp what is essentially human. One example of this is the pre-theoretical garbage-can model of Cohn, March & Olsen (1972). The tendency is also expressed in the demands of politicians and industry that we become more flexible and innovative, in production itself as well as in leadership. And this is due to the fact that such factors have, in recent years become parameters in industrial competition. In Denmark we will these years export the main portion of the systematisable work functions to, for instance, Poland, where labour is cheap. We maintain, however, and subsist on our innovation and production of individualised products, such as prototypes, and the performance of specialised services.

However, even though enterprises and institutions do have a great deal of experience in the areas of competence and leadership, neither the organisations nor the scientists have an exact conception of what competence is and how leadership should or can be practised. We know a considerable amount about qualifications, the development of qualifications and administration, but not a great deal about competence, the development of competence and leadership, a situation which it is, in my opinion, urgently necessary to do something about.

Literature

Ainsworth, N.D.S., & Bowlby, J. (1991). An ethological approach to personality development. *American Psychologist, 46*.
Bass, B.M. (1985). Leadership: Good, better best. *Organizational Dynamics, Winter.* 25-40.
Bennis, W. (1989). *Why leaders can't lead: the unconscious conspiracy continues.* San Francisco: Jossey-Bass.
Bennis, W.G., & Nanus, B (1985). *Leaders: the strategies for taking charge.* New York: Harper & Row.
Bierschenk, B. (1993). *The fundamentals of perspective text analysis.* Cognitive Science Research, no. 45. Lund University
Bierschenk, I. (1992). *An excursion into the ecological co-ordinates of language space.* Cognitive Science Research, no. 43. Lund University.
Blake, R.R., & Mouton, J.S. (1964). *The Managerial grid.* Houston, Tx: Gulf Publishing.
Bohm, D. (1990). *Wholeness and the implicate order.* London: Ark Paperbacks.
Bohm, D., & Hiley, B.J. (1993) *The undivided universe: An ontological interpretation of quantum theory.* London: Routledge.
Bowlby, J. (1969). *Attachment and loss. Vol. I. Attachment.* London: The Hogarth Press.
Burns, J.M. (1978). *Leadership.* New York: Harper & Row.
Chomsky, N. (1966). *Cartesian linguistics.* London: Harper & Row.
Cohn, M.D, March, J.G. & Olsen, J.P. (1972). A garbage can model of organisational choise. *Administrative Science Quarterly, 17,* 1-25.
Czarniawska-Joerges, B., & Wolff, R. (1991). Leaders, managers, entrepreneurs on and off the organizational stage. *Organization Studies, 12,4,* 529-546.
Elstrup Rasmussen, O. (1994a). *The discontinuity of human existence. Part I. The fundamental concepts of human existence and the relation between the singular and the super singular.* Cognitive Science Research, No. 50. Lund University.
Elstrup Rasmussen, O. (1994b). *The discontinuity of human existence. Part II. The general and the specific theories of discontinuity. Cognitive* Science Research, No. 51. Lund University.
Elstrup Rasmussen, O. (1994c). *The discontinuity of human existence. Part III. Perspective Text Analysis: A Methodological Approach to the Study of Competence.* Cognitive Science Research, No. 52. Lund University.
Fayol, H. (1949). *General and industrial management.* London: Isaac Pitman.
Fiedler, F.E. (1967). *A theory of leadership.* New York: McGraw-Hill.
French, J.R.P., & Raven, B. (1959). The bases of power. In: D. Cartwright (Ed.), *Studies in Social Power.* Ann Arbor: Univercity of Michigan.
Gartner, W.B. (1989). Who is an entrepreneur? Is the wrong question. *American Journal of Small Business,* 47-68.
Gibson, J. (1979). *The ecological approach to visual perception.* Boston: Houghton Mifflin.
Hersey, P., & Blanchard, K.H. (1988). *Management of organizational behavior.* Englewood Cliffs: Prentice-Hall.

Johnson, M. (1992). *The body in the mind. The bodily basis of meaning, imagination, and reason*. Chicago: The University of Chicago Press.

Kilby, I. (1971). Hunting the 'Heffalump'. In: I. Kilby (Ed.), *Entrepreneurship and economic development*. New York: Free Press.

Kugler, P.N., & Turvey, M.T.(1987). *Information., natural law and the assembly of rythmic movement*. London: Lawrence Erbaum.

McClelland, D.C. (1971). The two fases of power. In: D.A. Colb; I.M. Rubin, & J.M. Mcintyre (Eds.), *Organizational psychology*. Englewood Cliffs: Prentice-Hall.

McClelland, D.C. (1975). That urge to achieve. I: C.M. Baumback, & J.R. Mancuso (Eds.), *Entrepreneurship and venture management*. Englewood Cliffs: Printice-Hall.

Muczyk, J.P., & Reimann, B.C. (1987). The case for directive leadership. *Academy of Management Review, 12*, 637-647.

Nisbett, R. E. (Ed.) (1993). *Rules for reasoning*. Hillsdale: Lawrence Erlbaum.

Piaget, J. (1972). *Psykologi og erkendelsesteori (Psychology and epistemology)*. København: Hans Reitzel.

Prigogine, I, & Stengers, I. (1993). *Das Paradox der Zeit (The paradox of time)*. München: Piper.

Putnam, H. (1989). *Representation and reality*. Massachusetts: The MIT Press.

Schumpeter, J.A. (1931). *Theorie der wirtschaftlichen Entwicklung (The theory of economical development)*. München: Duncker & Humblot.

Stogdill, R.M. (1948). Personal factors associated with leadership: A survey of the litterature. *Journal of Psychology, 25*, 35-71.

Tarski, A. (1944). The semantic concept of truth. In: H. Feigel, & W. Sellars (Ed.), *Readings in philosophical analysis*. New York: Appelton Century Crofts

Taylor, F.W. (1916). *The principles of scientific management*. New York: Harper & Brothers Publishers.

Thom, R. (1975). *Structural stability and morphogenesis*. Massachusetts: Benjamin.

van de Ven, A.H. (1980). Early planning, implementation, and performance of new organizations. In: J. Kimberly, & R.H. Mills (Eds.), *The organizational life cycle*. London: Jossey-Bass.

Weber, M. (1972). *Wirtschaft und Gesellschaft (Economy and society)*. Tübingen: J.C.B. Mohr.

Yukl, G.A. (1994). *Leadership in organizations*. Englewood Cliffs: Printice-Hall.

Zaleznik, A. (1977). Managers and leaders: Are they different. *Harvard Business Review, 55*, 67-78.

Dream and Neuroses

ERIK SCHULTZ

From's book, *Dream and Neuroses*, first published in 1944, has this year been translated into English by Dr. Erik Kvan, Hong Kong. Academic circles in Denmark have for some time wanted to make this – fairly tiny – book accessible to a broader international public. In the English translation it covers 42 pages, in one sense a very modest publication indeed.

In another sense, the book is not modest at all. Although it has already reached the somewhat mature age of 51 years, it has during this time made a steadily growing impact on Danish psychology.

A critical voice might argue that the insight and ideas put forward in the book have been absorbed in to the tide of psychological research, so that the sting of many points is a little blurred.

Some theories developed after the Second World War advocate viewpoints similar to those of From. One could mention the construct theory of Kelly; the social constructionist line of thinking, the cognitive theory of Rosch, and some of the main points in hermeneutically inspired psychology.

However, the very fact that From's book suggests considerations that point in a direction capable of synthesizing viewpoints that were later to be developed in the abovementioned theoretical branches of psychology, enriches the book with a quality that speaks for itself.

Let us examine the ambition of the plot. From wants to comment on the insights of pychoanalytical thinking; but not in the way psychoanalysts understand themselves. No, From wants to comment on this by keeping strictly in line with the special phenomenological method that he, in a sense, was brought up with.

The title in itself – *Dream and Neuroses* – shows better that anything else that we are being invited to learn something about favourite themes of psychoanalysts. The subtitle is: "An Attempt at a New Point of View".

The new point of view is to consider the subtler sides of our mental life from a phenomenological position.

The Copenhagen Phenomenological School of Psychology

In the phenomenological method you are supposed to bracket metaphysical or ontological considerations altogether. Any old thing you may experience is regarded as an experience, whether it exists in reality or not. You may experience the lamp on your desk and you may experience a unicorn, and both experiences get the same status, although the first usually is considered to be an experience of a fact and the latter to be a hallucination. In the phenomenological method, however, you "forget" all about realities. The one and only reality you stick to is the experience as such.

Now, in some shools of phenomenology, this "reality bracketing" is regarded only as a methodological tool for getting in touch with the world of experiences. In the Copenhagen school of phenomenology the reality bracketing is carried further into a radical position. Here, one finds the viewpoint that it is in principle impossible to qualify experiences in terms of their reality status. The school therefore ends up in a kind of anti-ontological or even solipcistic position. The one and only thing we can know about is experience, and the question of reality vanishes.

This radical version of phenomenology is From's departure point, and it explains why the concept of "entity" becomes central in his book. We cannot know whether our focus of investigation is a real thing or a fantasy; so it is just "an entity".

Let us see where From wants to take us.

Processing and Subsumption

If the world is "nothing but experience", *perception* becomes the most important thing you can imagine, because it is the only "ontological" fact. As to perception, From follows the old tradition of distinguishing between "perception" and "apperception", but he prefers to rename these aspects in accordance with their nature.

The traditional "perception" is called (*sensory*) *processing* (*in Danish:* (sansemæssig) forarbejdning). The traditional "apperception" is renamed *subsumption* (indordning). "Processing" means that one or more sensory impacts, in co-operation with processes of the central nervous system make an experience. "Subsumption" implies that this experience is experienced as something definite.

From makes an important point by crossing "processing" and "subsumption" with "high" and "low". An example:

A town-dweller and a farmer are strolling down a track enjoying the scenery. The former perceives a "cornfield", while the latter perceives "barley". Now, the processing in both cases is high. They have a lot of time to focus on what they see, and they allow their senses and their central nervous systems to work out the experienced entities in a careful way.

Their subsumptions differ, nevertheless. The one subsumes the experience as "cornfield" while the latter subsumes it as "barley".

If the farmer had only had a tiny fraction of a second to look at the scenery, or if we had equipped him with very dark glasses, he might have experienced "cornfield" like the town-dweller. In this case the two persons' subsumptions would have matched each other, but for different reasons.

The town-dweller subsumed "cornfield" because his central nervous processes are unable to distinguish between "barley", "rye", "wheat" and "oats". These are the four types of grain grown in Denmark. Whatever is in the field, the town-dweller always experiences "cornfield", because the different sorts of crops are identical in his experience. A higher and more careful processing will not make any difference.

In contrast, to that the farmer's subsumption reaches a higher level, when his processing gets higher. We can see that higher processing may result in higher subsumption, but not always. Furthermore, low processing may occasionally result in very high subsumption. An example:

You sit in your office with the door open. Something out in the corridor hurries by, and that means that only a very low processing is possible. Usually you will have a low subsumption because of the poor processing conditions, you may experience "a person", "somebody", or even "a living creature", but you may also come up with a very high subsumption, "Mr Smith from department seven" .

Universalia, Identalia and Generalia
The notion of high and low processing and subsumption allows From to reconsider the traditional way of thinking about "concrete things" and "abstraction".

In medieval times a heavy dispute took place between "nominalists" and "realists".

A nominalist would claim that the abstract idea of, for example, "a horse" must be a subsumption we can make after we have experienced a lot of concrete horses. From experiences with many individual horses where no two of them were exactly identical, little by little we became able to grasp the *universal* notion of "horse".

A realist thinks otherwise. He will claim that we have a universal prototypical idea of "horse" that finds a concrete exemplification in the very particular jade in this very particular field.

One could say – although From does not mention it – that the realist position in medieval times is very much the Platonic kind of objective idealism. A universal idea throws its impact on chaotic experiences and provides order for our perceptions. And the realist position is of course also very comparable to the Kantian notion of "inborn categories". In fact, the position is comparable to all kinds of rationalism.

The nominalist position is, on the other hand, very comparable to all kinds of "empiristic" positions in science and philosophy. From claims that his perceptual terminology is capable of solving the dispute between nominalists and realists – and thereby between rationalists and empirists one might add; a solution that can also synthesize the psychoanalytical and phenomenolocial positions.

The "concrete entities" that the nominalists (and empirists) want us to experience before we can get hold of an "abstract universal idea" are not more or less concrete than anything else we experience. And the "abstract universal ideas" are not more or less abstract than anything else. From holds that our experienced entities always place themselves between two different kinds of universals or *universalia*. The first kind of "universalia" he calls *identalia*. An example:

The town-dweller who has optimal processing conditions in his perception, and experiences an entity where barley, oats, wheat and rye are "one and the same entity" – namely "cornfield" – experiences an identalia. He is not making an abstraction based on "four different particular kinds of cornfields". The farmer, on the other hand, who is able to subsume the four kind of "cornfields" as four different kinds of entity, is also able to make a universalia based on these. He may very well be able to subsume all four types as "crop". This kind of universalia is by From called a *generalia*. From therefore holds that the nominalists (empirists) are right in claiming that "universal categories" are based on concrete experiences with particulars. The nominalists are right as long as we are dealing with generalia.

On the other hand the realists (rationalists) are right in claiming that "universal categories" come before particulars. They are right as long as we are dealing with identalia.

And this has prepared us to look a little closer at children's experiences, dreams, neurotic experiences and "primitive" people's experiences.

Identalia as a key to understanding the unconscious

According to From, our perceptions in daily life, under conditions where we are fully awake and clearminded, will consist of experienced entities that we are able to distinguish and generalia-categorize.

We may experience "a blackbird" and a "sparrow" on the lawn (entities we can distinguish) but we may also experience "two birds" (generalia). There was a time, however, when we could not distinguish these two animals from each other. In fact, there may have been a time when birds and other animals were subsumed as "one and the same thing". Maybe it was so in our early childhood. If so, the two "birds" on the lawn would not have been "birds" at all, because this is a generalia category. The two "birds" would nevertheless have been subsumed as "one and the same thing", but now as an identalia category.

Small children are busy learning their language, and they have to deal with the categories of the adults' language, categories that mirror the distinctions and generalia categories ordinary grown-ups are capable of using. Children have to deal with the words "sparrow", "blackbird" and "bird". The grown-ups point at the birds and say with enthusiasm to the children: "Look, there is a sparrow and a blackbird" or: "Look, there are two birds".

Now, if the entity experienced by the child covers what the grown-ups call birds, mammals, cartoon-figures and dolls, the child learns to connect the words "sparrow", "blackbird" and "bird" with this identalia category. Therefore, children often use language in a surprising way. They may point to a doll and say, e.g., "blackbird".

Apparently nobody ever taught them this, but the experienced identalia category that covers blackbirds as well as dolls does the trick. Is it possible that the experienced identalia categories of early childhood "are still with us"?, that they are "with us" in the sense that we fall back on them when unconcentrated and when dreaming.

From thinks so, and he offers a lot of examples. When unconcentrated we may show our bus ticket when we enter the cinema. Why? Because "going into a place where one has to show a ticket" is an identalia category that governs the experience while unconcentrated.

Dreaming in our sleep about our teacher of mathematics, who at the same time is – or suddenly becomes – the actual boss at our work, is understandable if an identalia category that we might call "superior person that gives us problems", is subsuming our experience.

From's main point as to psychoanalysis is that we should not consider our unconscious experiences as a messed-up version of our usual categories. Rather, the so-called unconscious consists of identalia categories that once upon a time, in our early days, were the very categories we had to subsume with under even the highest processing.

The town-dweller could not distinguish the four kind of crops as could the farmer, but he could certainly learn to do so easily. His identalia category are open to differentiation. Open to differentiation is also the unconcentrated man's identalia category "going into a place where one has to show a ticket", he just has to concentrate his mind. Open to differentiation is also the dreamers identalia category "superior person that gives us problems"; he just has to wake up.

From holds that such undeveloped identalia categories are our phenomenologically given experiences in relaxed, unrestrained states of mind as well as in dreaming when asleep. Usually, these categories will be transformed to more differentiated identalia categories when allowed the thorough processing that the awake, concentrated mind offers.

He suggest further that neurotics may have identalia categories at work that resist the usual differentiation typical of the awake, concentrated mind, maybe because a painful conflict is avoided by keeping early identalia categories in charge. Therefore, the resistant identalia categories persist in neurotic symptoms.

Finally, From suggests that his viewpoint may have some interesting points to make about so-called "primitive" people's categories, and he touches upon the possibility of understanding the structure of language in terms of identalia categories on various levels.

From Emotional Dynamism to Cognition

No doubt From is a theorist who places himself as a frontal figure in the traditions that want to exchange the psychoanalytical understanding of unconscious life as an emotional dynamism with a cognitive approach. It is, according to From, the structure of our cognitive categories that is the path to follow, if we are to succeed in understanding "the themes from psychoanalysis" in a scientific way.

Many have followed this path after From, and for all interested in this approach From has a lot of interesting things to say, not least when one takes into account the strict phenomenological example From gives us. We are, through the whole book, in comfortable contact with examples which are easy for anybody to comprehend, and From enriches his phenomenological viewpoint with a pleasant style of writing that supports his message.

Should one want to make a few remarks from the middle nineties – about fifty years later than the birth of the book – two aspects might be worth considering. One is to point out that From maybe misses some of the emotional depths that psychoanalysis has taught us about. The nervous symptoms may very well be understood as identalia categories resistant to the usual differential power of awake, concentrated efforts, but why are the categories resisting? Why cannot the neurotic solve the painful problems in the usual, mature way? One may feel a litte let down on that problem.

The other is to notice how From has problems with the strict Copenhagen phenomenological vision of refraining from all ontological or metaphysical speculation. From claims very persistently that he sticks to the world's appearance in experience. What really is in the world is not considered as a fruitful question.

On page 39, where From comments on the nominalist/realist dispute, he says:

> "Without in any way attempting to take sides regarding the metaphysical content of the debate about what "really exists", we shall try to look at thepsychological antecedents of the two views".

From then synthesizes the two views and claims right on both sides as described earlier. However, on page 3 From says (authors emphasis):

> "But in our environment nothing exists *except changing atomic vibration*, or whatever it is, which stimulates our sensory organs in different ways, and only through our processing of these stimulations does the experience arise".

The present author has in various papers (e.g., Schultz, 1988) made a thorough criticism of the position where one refrains from ontological considerations. It is simply impossible to do so. Notice how From, in the first quote, rejects taking a stand in such considerations, while he in the latter quote does so anyhow. Here he allows "atomic vibration" to be the one and only existing reality in the world, whereas all the rest is experiences that we make out of these vibrations by processing and subsumption.

By radicalizing the phenomenological position, From – as well as other adherents of Copenhagen phenomenology – suddenly finds himself in an ontological position where "atomic vibrations" are realities and anything else mind creations, but where should one find a satisfying explanation for this? If "anything else" is mind creations, why on earth are "atomic vibrations" then not mind creations?

The problem is that the processing mind has to have something to process. It cannot process stimulation that is mind-made concepts. Therefore the principle of refraining from the ontological problem is born to self-contradiction, and it hits From's point of view in an interesting way. From's message is very apt in describing people's different categorial ways of experiencing the world, but it cannot discuss the question of wrong and right perceptions. In the example with the farmer and the town-dweller we saw different categorisation, but both persons were right. The one experienced "cornfield", the other "barley".

Now, if one of the persons – e.g., the town-dweller – had experienced "rye", he would have been wrong in his experience. From's ontological nihilism forces him to accept any experience being as good as any other, a consequence that is probably in line with From's viewpoint, but is it a position that can be defended? And how does he manage to hold this viewpoint and at the same time, in a self contradictory way, promote the nuclear world as the one and only ontological reality?

In spite of these critical remarks, From's little book has an impressive quality as an overture to various cognitive reconsiderations on psychoanalysis.

References

Schultz, E (1988): *Personlighedspsykologi på erkendelsesteoretisk grundlag.* Copenhagen; Dansk Psykologisk Forlag.

From, Franz (1944): *Dream and Neuroses.* Dansk Psykologisk Forlag 1995.

Identity, Self-Concept and Sport

The Development of a Theory of the Self and its Evaluation by Multiple Case Study Research in Different Sport Settings

REINHARD STELTER

Social changes have an influence on the body and movement culture of our society and on psychological factors in relation to body experience and body impression management. On the one hand, sport and movement activities are the basis of specific bodily experiences, and these experiences have a fundamental meaning for the athletes' self-concept or the personal construction of the self. On the other hand, involvement in a specific kind of sport setting is the manifestation of an impression-management strategy which is related to the person's attempt to develop, personal lifestyle. In that sense, the choice of the social setting, in casu the choice of a specific sport setting, is a strategy adopted by the individual in relation to the social construction of the self.

Because of the lack of a well-developed psychological theory of identity which can include the bodily perspective for the construction of the self, a theory of the self on the basis of five different dimensions is proposed:

1. *The body self* evolves from bodily perceptions of the world around us. On the basis of these perceptions, the lived-in body is a mediator between the person and the world.
2. *The self as a personal construction or the self-concept* is an emotional-cognitive structure. Through the process of perception we create our personal reality.
3. *The self as a social construction or the self as relational*: Our personal constructions have to be defended and have to be intelligible in the social context. Identity has to be *negotiated*. There are three major strategies in this process: a) *The language discourse*, b) *impression management* and c) *choice of social setting*.

4. *Developmental orientation in relation to self constructions* (personal biography).
5. *Socio-historical orientation in relation to self constructions* (cultural relativism).

This theory of the self is an attempt to combine a phenomenological approach (i.e. Merleau-Ponty) with a social constructionist one (i.e. Gergen).

The empirical part of the research is based on participant observation and in-depth interviews with twenty sports people (ten of each sex) in different sport settings: Tennis as service-orientated leisure time sport (pilot study), medium and long-distance running as a top elite sport, soccer as sport-for-all and competitive orientated sport, and aerobics/weightlifting as a commercial sport in a fitness centre. The results are presented in four single-case analyses and in several cross-case analyses. The research findings of the cross-case analyses can be presented as follows:

1. *Body experience is a unique entrance to the life world of sports participants.* Independently of the setting, sports people perceive themselves and their bodies mainly in a positive way ("easiness", "energy", "unification with the environment", "euphoria"). A lot of the categories found can be related to the concept of *flow* described by Czikszentmihalyi (1975). In that sense, sport can be described as an autotelic activity. Negative emotions are mainly related to the perception of failure in competitive situations.
2. *"Perceived self-efficacy"* (Bandura 1986) – *a feeling of "I can do it" – is a phenomenon experienced by all sports participants.* In relation to other life situations, sport can be defined as a simply structured social system that makes it very easy for the individual to perceive self-efficacy.
3. *Sports participants develop identity according to the sport setting chosen by them.*
   Sports people stabilize their identity (among other things) by seeking the specific sport setting that best fits their self-concept and that offers self-confirmatory feedback. The chosen sport setting can be understood as an identity-stabilizing social situation. In that sense, choice of setting is part of the social construction of the self.

In the three different sport settings which are included in the cross-case analyses, the sports people negotiate their identities as follows: a) For the medium and long-distance runners in the field of top elite sport, *"the optimal use of their own resources"* is the major identity theme in relation to their sport; b) For the soccer players in a sport-for-all and competitively orientated setting, the *team* or the *social group* is the central reference point for their identity negotiations; c) For the sports people in the commercial fitness centre, *"self-control"* is the major identity theme in relation to their sport.

Because of the well-defined social environment, the results of this research can be transformed theoretically to other areas of personal and social psychology.

The research is published in German and Danish:
Stelter, R. (in print). *Du bist wie dein Sport. Studien zu Selbstkonzept- und Identititätsentwicklung.* Schorndorf: Hofmann.
Stelter, R. (1995). *Oplevelse & iscenesættelse – identitetsudvikling i idrætten.* Copenhagen/Herning: DHL-Forlaget/forlaget systime.

Reference:
Czikszentmihalyi, M. (1975) *Beyond Boredom and Anxiety.* San Francisco: Jossoy-Bass.

Reinhard Stelter works at *Danish State Institute of Physical Education, University of Copenhagen.*

Psycho-social practice

MORTEN NISSEN

In today's sociology and social psychology there is a growing emphasis on discrete forms of organized social action rather than abstract notions of properties of "the" society or "the" individual. Reflections of local development projects as agents of theoretical research connect to ideas of action research from the 1970s. As what may be the other side of this coin, critique of ideology in abstract terms is gradually being replaced by a more historically differentiated study of the discourses that unfold in everyday life modes and in organized fields of practice such as medicine, psychology, etc. The aim of my present research is to bring together these approaches in studies of development projects in the field of psycho-social work.

This research is intimately connected both to programme evaluation efforts and to theoretical development efforts (at the Psychological Laboratory and in the multi-disciplinary research project "Health, Man and Culture", which resides in Aarhus University) towards a general model of action contexts. As a general conceptual framework I seek to continue the dialectical materialist tradition growing from activity theory (Vygotsky, Leontiev etc.) into the general science of the subject that has been presented as "Critical Psychology" (cf. Holzkamp, Osterkamp, Dreier etc.), while integrating approaches and notions developed in the more semiotic trends such as ethnomethodology (Garfinkel, etc.), symbolic interactionism, systems theory, or social constructionism.

A general account of this line of work is represented in my book (in Danish) "User influence and action contexts in psycho-social practice", accepted as a PhD thesis in November 1994 (with an English summary). The thesis starts out from the assumption that the concept of user influence and user perspectives research tends to merge with forms of discourse and practice that prevail as individual autonomy and general qualifications gradually become the dominant form of societal integration. What was meant to empower turns out to individualize. In co-operation with development projects, however, I also hypothesized notions of how action contexts may be constructed to overcome this paradox.

Some development projects that organize voluntary social work on an ideological basis may be viewed as self-sustaining cultural entities, which we may term local cultures because they seem to establish, reproduce and develop themselves as coherent cultures through the local form of an evolving organization. The fact that what is organized is not merely goal-oriented work, but includes the structuring and interpretation of everyday life, opens important perspectives regarding marginalization and integration. Yet we are dealing with a genuine social agent with a will of its own, not merely a "community" in the abstract and vague sense prevalent in social work discourse. Given certain conditions, the local culture project can utilize economic surplus (in the form of manpower, financial grants, etc.) to reintegrate socially excluded individuals and groups, while at the same time advancing "user influence" towards a practice that organizes a collective narrative of the self. In this way, the often idiosyncratic meanings and reasons for action of the marginalized may prove possible to include, not in a futile, self-referring discourse, as in the psycho-therapeutic context that tends to eliminate subjectivity by the management of its interpretation, but in a practice which responds to practical forms and implications of social exclusion.

In the thesis, the practical discourse on personality and the contradictions which result from the clash with traditional workings of the social system are reflected in the movements of concrete contexts of action. Finally, the unfolding of the co-operative development and research project is reflected in terms of a general methodology that points to the relevance and consistency of general concepts introduced and transformed as references in a local joint venture.

The works of Kurt Goldstein

BJARNE PEDERSEN

pp. 186 + Goldstein-bibliography, pp. 41. University of Copenhagen, Faculty of the Humanities, Psychological Laboratory, 1995.

The Ph.D. thesis can be summarized as an analysis and evaluation of *Kurt Goldstein's* scientific works.

The dissertation begins with a Foreword (Chapter I) in which it is explained why the author chose Goldstein as a subject of study. After the Foreword, the Introduction (Chapter II) follows. Here it is stated that the intention is to write a monograph, not a biography, about Goldstein. The project is defined from a history of science perspective, which in this context means aspects of the history of *neuropsychology*. The chapter concludes with an outline of the methodology. The third chapter contains a list of the cardinal years of school, university, and professional appointments of Goldstein.

Goldstein's writings can be divided into three main periods: Before World War I (I.), from World War I until he was expelled from Germany in 1933 (II.), and the later, approximately thirty years in the USA (III.). The order of the following three chapters reflects this division.

In Main Period I., i.e., before the First World War, Goldstein worked with a wide variety of problems within neuromedicine, e.g., morphogenetic and neuroanatomical investigations, including studies of CNS pathology; and diseases such as aphasia, apraxia, hallucinations and memory also attracted his attention. At this early stage of his scientific career he had already discovered 'holistic' traits, for instance, in the morphogenesis of the brain and, especially, in the functioning of the glandular system. He also started to 'use', i.e., apply the psychology of his time to explain some of the sequelae following brain damage (for example aphasia). These topics make up the content of Chapter IV.

Main Period II. (reviewed in Chapter V) is the most important and – from a psychological point of view – the most interesting part of Goldstein's professional life. On the basis of examinations of brain-damaged soldiers he developed a new theory concerning the dynamics of the brain. The so-called 'localization-theory' of his time, claiming 'centers' distributed all over the cortex 'containing' different well-defined specific functions, was proven to be incorrect. On the contrary, the brain works as a functional whole. Even specific functions always involve the whole brain: For instance, visual perception cannot be 'located' in the (primary) visual cortex in the occipital lobes alone, as the whole brain – in principle – takes part. Consequently, a seemingly circumscribed function is, in fact, only a *special* manifestation of a more basic form of functioning of the nervous system, which is expected to occur through a so-called figure/ground process. The figure/ground interaction is a Gestalt phenomenon. According to Goldstein, therefore, cerebral functioning is, in principle, comprehensible within the frame of reference of Gestalt psychology.

Physiological and psychological functioning are manifestations of the same basic form of functioning, according to Goldstein, hence the structure of the latter can be understood by analysing the structure of the former. Since they have the same origin, it is supposed that the laws from the psychological 'sphere' can be applied in the physiological 'sphere', and vice versa. Therefore, psychological Gestalt laws can be used in the understanding of the brain's physiological functioning. The functional holistic approach is also used in understanding and explaining dysfunctions following braindamage, for instance the catastrophic reaction. Rehabilitation, therefore, is also carried out within a holistic frame of reference.

In the sixth chapter Goldstein's scientific innovations in the USA are mentioned (Main Period III.). Although most of his original thinking had been done in Germany, the idea of self-actualisation was new. Furthermore, the concepts of abstract and concrete behavior were clarified. He also published (together with Scheerer) a psychological test concerning the latter.

In Chapter VII and VIII the Conclusion and Summary (in English) respectively appear.

A complete list of Goldstein's published writings makes up the content of Chapter IX. The bibliography consists of 366 items divided into eleven categories, i.e. a) books, b) monographs, c) articles, d) papers, e) summaries of papers, f) comments, g) abstracts, h) works edited by Goldstein, i) obituaries (of other scientists), j) reviews, and k) works of Goldstein & one or more co-writer(s).

The last Chapter X is the reference list. Two appendices end the dissertation. The first of these is a photocopy of an SS/Nazi document briefly describing the reasons for Goldstein's imprisonment and expatriation, the second is a Summary in Danish of the Ph.D. thesis.

PUBLICATIONS 1994-1995
BY RESEARCHERS AT PSYCHOLOGICAL
LABORATIRY & İNSTITUTE OF CLINICAL PSYCHOLOGY
UNIVERSITY OF COPENHAGEN

Aboulafia, A. & Hammond, N.
(1994) Notes from Session S8, Barcelona: Evaluation of designers fromm Praxis, Bath. In: *ESPRIT Basic Research Action 7040: AMODEUS, PRESS8.*

Aboulafia, A., Klausen, T., Jørgensen, A.H.
(1994) Towards a Theoretical Underpining of Scenarios. In: *Proceedings of the 17th Information Systems Research Seminar (IRIS) in Scandinavia, Part II. University of Oulu, Finland.*

Aboulafia, A.
(1995) Activity Theory – A way forward in HCI. In: *ESPRIT Basic Research Action 7040: AMODEUS, TA/WP24.*

Aboulafia, A., Gould, E., Spyrou, T.
(1995) Activity Theory vs. Cognitive Science in the study of Human Computer Interaction. In: *Proceedings of the 18th Information Systems Research Seminar in Scandinavia (IRIS'95). Gjern Feriecenter, Denmark, August 11-13, 1995. Part I, pp 29-38. Gothenburg Studies in Informatics, Report 7, June 1995,* 9 p.

Aboulafia, A. & Gould, E.
(1995) Information Processing vs. Human Cognition: A Critical Review of Cognitive Approaches in IT and HCI. In: *Proceedings of the International Society for the System Sciences (IRRS), the 39th annual meeting, Free University, Amsterdam 24th-28th July, 1995.*

Aboulafia, A., Blandford, A.E. et al.
(1995) Integration Techniques for Multi-Disciplinary HCI Modelling: A Survey. In: *ESPRIT Basic Research Action 70040: AMODEUS.*

Aboulafia, A. & Klausen, T.
(1995) Research into designers use of scenarios. In: *CHI'95 Research Symposium. Conference Companion Proceedings of CHI'95.* Denver, Colorado USA.

Aboulafia, A., Jørgensen, A. Helms et al.
(1995) Transfer and Assay of the Guide 'Designers Displays': A Preliminary Report. In: *ESPRIT Basic Research Action 7040: AMODEUS, TA/WP35.*

Almstrup, O.
(1994) *Resistance and Countertransference in Psychoanalytic Child Psychotherapy.* First European Conference of Psychoanalytic Child and Adolescent Psychotherapy, Athens May 1994.

Axel, E.
(1994) *Giving Tools Meaning within the Organization of Concrete Work Situation.* Paper to Social Science Research, Technical Systems and Cooperative Work. Published by Departement Sciences Humaines et Sociales, CNRS, Paris 1993.

Barnard, P.J., Bernsen, N.O., Jørgensen, A. Helms m.fl.
(1995) Final Report: Assaying Means of Design Expressions for users and systems. In: *AMODEUS Report D13.* 43 p.

Beckmann, J. & Hutchings, B.
(1994) *Conflict and Mental Health.* Report

Bjerg, K.
(1994) A presentation of the Experimentel Home of the 90's. In: K. Bjerg & Kim Borreby (eds.) *HOIT 94, Proceedings of Intl. Cross-disciplinary Conf. "Home-Oriented Informatics, Telematics & Automation".* København, Psykologisk Laboratorium p. 1-7.

Bjerg, K.
(1994) Domestic Information Dynamics and the Virtual Home. In: K. Bjerg & Kim Borreby (eds.) *HOIT 94, Proceedings of Intl. Cross-disciplinary Conf. "Home-Oriented Informatics, Telematics & Automation".* København, Psykologisk Laboratorium.

Bjerg, K. & Borreby, K (eds.)
(1994) *HOIT 94, Proceedings of Intl. Cross-disciplinary Conference "Home-Oriented Informatics, Telematics & Automation".* København, Psykologisk Laboratorium.

Bjerg, K.
(1994) Private Homes and Neighbourhoods: Agenda for a Long-Term Information Technology Policy. In: K. Bjerg & Kim Borreby (eds.) *HOIT 94, Proceedings of Intl. Cross-disciplinary Conf. "Home-Oriented Informatics, Telematics & Automation"*. København, Psykologisk Laboratorium.

Boman, K., Strandbygaard, B. & Vestergaard-Bogind, J.
(1994) *The Selfproject, preliminary results*. 16th International Congress of psychotherapy. Seoul, august, 17 p.

Buch, T., Ødum, J. & Jørgensen, A. Helms
(1995) Exploring the Use of Ideal Speech Recognition. Report.

Buckingham Shum, S., Jørgensen, A. Helms, Hammond, N. & Aboulafia, A.
(1994) *Amodeus HCI modelling and design approaches: Executive summaries and worked examples*. 500 p.

Buckingham Shum, S., Jørgensen, A. Helms, Hammond, N. & Aboulafia, A.
(1994) *Communicating and evaluating HCI Modelling: Analysing the ISLE Hypermedia system*. 45 p.

Buckingham Shum, S., Jørgensen, A. Helms, Aboulafia, A. & Nick, H.
(1994) Communication HCI modelling to Practitioners. In: *Adjunct Proc. CHI'94 Human Factors in Computing Systems, Boston, april 1994* p. 271-272.

Bundesen, C.
(1994) A computational theory of selective attention in vision. *Biologiske skrifter* 43, p. 167-178.

Bundesen, C. & Shibuya, H. (eds.)
(1995) *Visual Selective Attention: A Special Issue of the Journal Visual Cognition*. Hove, Lawrence Erlbaum Associates Ltd. 288 p.

Bundesen, C. & Shibuya, H.
(1995) Visual Selective Attention: Editors' Introduction. *Visual Cognition* 2, p. 97-100.

Christensen, A. & Teasdale, T.W.
(1994) Family reactions to experienced changes in the patient. *Giornale Italiano di Medicina Riabilitata* 8, p. 242-246.

Dreier, O.
(1994) Personal locations and perspectives – psychological aspects of social practice. *Psychological Yearbook* 1, p. 63-90.

Engelsted, N. & Køppe, S.
(1994) Putting Copenhagen psychology on the map. *Psychological Yearbook* 1, p. 9-26.

Engelsted, N.
(1994) Sense and Significance in Phylogenetic Reconstruction. *Mind, Culture, Activity* 1,1/2, p. 107-118.

Gade, A.
(1994) Imagery as a mnemonic aid in amnesia patients: effects of amnesia subtypes and severity. In: *Cognitive Neuropsychology and Cognitive Rehabilitation*. p. 571-589.

Gammelgaard, J.
(1994) Psychoanalysis and classical tragedy. *Psychological Yearbook* 1, p. 27-45.

Gammelgaard, J.
(1995) The tragic emotions. In press, *Scandinavian Journal of Psychoanalysis*.

Hammond, N., Buckingham Shum, S., Jørgensen, A. Helms & Abouulafia, A.
(1994) *S-Transferring and assaying HCI modelling and Design approaches*. 111 p.

Jørgensen, A. Helms & Aboulafia, A.
(1994) *Perception of Design Rationale*.Report, 6 p.

Jørgensen, A. Helms & Aboulafia, A.
(1994) Transfer and assay: Concerns and commitments. In: *ESPRIT Basic Research Action 7040: AMODEUS, TA/WP27*. 10 p.

Jørgensen, A. Helms & Aboulafia, A.
(1995) Perceptions of Design Rationale. In: K. Norby, P.H.Helmersen, D.J.Gilmore & S.A.Arnesen (eds.) *Human Computer Interaction: Interact 95* London, Chapman and Hall, p. 61-66.

Klausen, T., Aboulafia, A., Jørgensen, A. Helms
(1994) Towards a theoretical underpinning of scenarios. In: *Proc. 17th IRIS.*

Klausen, T. & Aboulafia, A.
(1995) An Empirical Study of Professional Software Designers use of scenarios. In: *Proceedings of the OZCHI 95 Conference, HCI – A light into the future. University of Wollongong, Dept. of Business Systems, Australia (Nov 27-30, 1995).*

Kuschel, R.
(1994) *Homicide and Blood Feuds on a Polynesian Outlier.* Polish Academy of Sciences, 34 p.

Kuschel, R.
(1994) Killing begets killing: Homicides and Blood Feuds on a Polynesian Outlier. *Bijdragen* 149, 4, p. 690-717.

Kuschel, R.
(1994) *Managing Martial Conflicts on Bellona Island.* 2nd International European Conference of Oceanist, Basel, 31 p.

Kuschel, R.
(1994) *Managing Martial Conflicts on Bellona Island.* International Conference on Violence in the Family, Amsterdam, 31 p.

Kuschel, R.
(1994) *Qualitative Methods in the Social Sciences.* Save the Children Fund, Chautara, Nepal, 243 p.

Kuschel, R. & Willerup, S.
(1994) That's Enough! Succesful strategies in counteracting violence in Danish Municipolities. In: J. M. Ramirez (eds.) *Violence: Some alternatives* Madrid, Centreur.

Larsen, A. & Bundesen, C.
(1994) *Mental Translation in Visual Space.* Report, 11 p.

Leth, I.
(1994) *Child Sexual Abuse.* Report.

Mørch, S.
(1994) Une Théorie de la Jeunesse. In: R. Hudan & B. Fournier (eds.) *Jeunesse et politique.* Paris, L'Harmattan, p. 73-108.

Nielsen, J. & Aboulafia, A.
(1994) Embedding Design in Activity Theory CHI'94 Research Symposium. In: *Conference Companion Proceedings of CHI'94.* New York, ACM.

Nielsen, J. & Aboulafia, A.
(1994) The Qualified Designer – Embedding Design in Activity Theory. In: *ESPRIT Basic Research Action 7040: AMODEUS, TA/WP18.*

Petersen, A. Friemuth
(1994) Biopsychological aspects of individuation: on the origin of and interplay between biological individuality, personality and self. *Psychological Yearbook* 1, p. 45-62.

Petersen, A. Friemuth
(1994) Some Reflections on Motivating Situations and Situational Teaching. *Scandinavian Journal of Educational Research* 38, 3-4, p. 267-278.

Petersen, A. Friemuth
(1995) *Emergence of speech in autistic children: From stereotypy and echolalia to rituals and speech acts* Invited paper at the International Workshop on "Speech Motor Control and Stuttering", Centro Medico di Riabiliazione, Veruno, 26th-27h May 1995, 10 p.

Petersen, A. Friemuth
(1995) *Speaking against Lipsius: On problems of identity in studies of biological, psychological and socio-cultural phenomena.* Paper given at the International "Workshop on Ethnic Identity: Psychological and Anthropological Perspectives", Inst. of Child and Adolescent Psychiatry, Karasjok 12th – 14th Jan 1995.

Petersen, A. Friemuth
(1995) Sur le regard interactif chez l'enfant de 7 à 27 mois dans des situations d'initiation et de conflit. *Les cahiers du Cerfee, Montpellier* 11-12, p. 145-155.

Poulsen, Annette
(1994) Cognitive aspects and existential themes in group therapy. *Scandinavian Journal of Psychology* 27, p. 1-40.